THE KEY TO YOUR FUTURE IS IN YOUR MOUTH

BY BISHOP CLIFTON JONES

Copyright © 2010 by Bishop Clifton Jones

The Key To Your Future Is In Your Mouth
by Bishop Clifton Jones

Printed in the United States of America

ISBN 9781609571177

All rights reserved solely by the author. The author guarantees all contents are original and do not infringe upon the legal rights of any other person or work. No part of this book may be reproduced in any form without the permission of the author. The views expressed in this book are not necessarily those of the publisher.

Unless otherwise indicated, Bible quotations are taken from The King James Version. Copyright © 1988-2002 by Bible Soft Program.

www.xulonpress.com

This book is dedicated to my pastor Elder Stanley S. Jones Sr., and his wife Marian, two people that seemed to have enjoyed every lesson that was taught and the sermons that were preached. Your encouraging words were greatly appreciated.

Thank you Pastor Jones for assuming the role of caring for the saints at Jerusalem Temple. The place where I was blessed to spend 40 years. You are doing a fine job working with the people that I love and care much for.

May the good Lord continue to give you grace to work with His people, while seeking to prepare them for His soon return.

TABLE OF CONTENTS

GOD'S WORD SETS THE PATTERN 13
GOD'S WORD IS THE KEY TO OUR
    POSITIVE CONVERSATION 23
THE WAY TO LIFE AND GOOD DAYS 31
WATCH WHAT YOU SAY 45
DON'T JUST LISTEN YOU NEED TO TALK 64
TURNING THINGS AROUND WITH
    RIGHT WORDS 88
GETTING BACK TO GOD WITH RIGHT
    WORDS 99
TONGUE CONTROL A SIGN OF
    STRENGTH 109
SOME WORDS ANNOY GOD BUT SOME
    ARE PLEASING TO HIM. 122
THE QUESTION OF THE HOUR 155
VOICE ACTIVATION 174
LET YOUR VOICE BE HEARD 193

INTRODUCTION

I trust that none of us will take lightly the message of this book because the tongue is a wonderful instrument, that is, when it is used according to its creative purpose. However, if the tongue is used wrongly, it is sure to cause many hurts and harm.

I trust that something said in this book will awaken, warn and educate your mind and spirit and put you on the alert, so that life and good will proceed out of your mouth. It would be wonderful for all believers to dedicate their tongues to the life-giving ministry, because we have more than enough life-killing tongues on the loose.

The tongue is a strong indicator of one's spiritual maturity and self-discipline. It is also the channel that flows from the heart.

The tongue leaves little to doubt about what's in one's heart, it is known to speak the language that the heart contains.

We often hear that one can't tell what's in a person's heart. According to the Word of God, all one would have to do is stick around a while and what's in the heart will soon proceed out of the mouth.

The Lord, our creator, was the first to demonstrate the power of the tongue when He spoke the world into existence. The times He used His mouth to proclaim victory in advance, He left us an example on the creative use of the tongue.

We should capitalize on the many divine examples left in the Word of God. I feel reasonably sure that He wants us to make the best use of the tongue.

No doubt you have heard the tongue used wrongly many times. You have heard it curse, lie, criticize, gossip, backbite, murmur and complain. These are improper ways to use the tongue for a believer.

The correct way to use the tongue is to speak life, speak good and glorify the name of the Lord.

We are also told to encourage one another. Your mouth can speak life, motivation, encouragement and strength into the life of a person.

Let us not forget that it was God's plan that preaching should be the method used to save the lost and guess what, the mouth is the instrument that is used to do the speaking.

I confess, I had a wonderful time putting together this material. I found it to be refreshing, inspirational, and enlightening to the spirit to see the many times the Bible speaks about the tongue, mouth and voice.

May you find that which would benefit you the most in your search to maintain a quality life of holiness and righteousness before the presence of the living God.

GOD'S WORD SETS THE PATTERN

When you read the book called the Bible you are sure to see that the words mouth, lips, tongue, voice, speech, sayings and related terms dominate the pages. The reason these terms are so prevalent in the Bible is that they play a major role in the outcome of one's life, future, hope, happiness and success.

The tongue was used in the creation of this vast universe. God spoke into existence the things which were made, we see in Genesis the first chapter that **"God said"**.

"And God said, Let there be light: and there was light." (Gen 1:3 KJV)

> "And God said, Let there be a firmament in the midst of the waters, and let it divide the waters from the waters." (Gen 1:6 KJV)
>
> "And God said, Let the waters under the heaven be gathered together unto one place, and let the dry land appear: and it was so." (Gen 1:9 KJV)
>
> "And God said, Let the earth bring forth grass, the herb yielding seed, and the fruit tree yielding fruit after his kind, whose seed is in itself, upon the earth: and it was so." (Gen 1:11 KJV)
>
> "And God said, Let there be lights in the firmament of the heaven to divide the day from the night; and let them be for signs, and for seasons, and for days, and years:" (Gen 1:14 KJV)

I think you get the picture, God used His mouth to create the things that were made. When God made man, He breathed into man life; again He used His mouth.

> "And the LORD God formed man of the dust of the ground, and breathed into his nos-

> **trils the breath of life; and man became a living soul." (Gen 2:7 KJV)**

God's word, is breath or Spirit, contains life. When He speaks to something, life commences in that thing or person.

Jesus said it best when He spoke to His followers on the subject of life and spirit. He wanted them to know that the words that He spoke contained life. His words had creative power to bring about change.

> **"It is the spirit that quickeneth; the flesh profiteth nothing: the words that I speak unto you, they are spirit, and they are life." (John 6:63 KJV)**

It is to our advantage to pay close attention to the emphasis that Jesus places on the words that He speaks because they are life giving. The life giving power that is in the Word of God does not diminish when God's word is spoken by a believer because it is God's word and not just the words of the one that speaks.

It is a must that every believer store in his or her heart the Word of God because the word is inseparable from the God that spoke the word. One that has the Word of God has the God that spoke the word. That is why the Apostle Peter spoke confidently that staying with Jesus would be the thing to do because He had the life giving word.

> *"Then Simon Peter answered him, Lord, to whom shall we go? thou hast the words of eternal life." (John 6:68 KJV)*

We must come to grips that God's word is eternal, and we should look upon it as living and eternal. Everything that the Lord has spoken is already settled. We must strive to make sure that it is settled in us because the word will not change, but it will change us because it is alive.

> **"The law of the LORD is perfect, converting the soul: the testimony of the LORD is sure, making wise the simple.**
> **8 The statutes of the LORD are right, rejoicing the heart: the commandment of the LORD is pure, enlightening the eyes.**

9 The fear of the LORD is clean, enduring for ever: the judgments of the LORD are true and righteous altogether.

10 More to be desired are they than gold, yea, than much fine gold: sweeter also than honey and the honeycomb." (Ps 19:7-10 KJV)

Our desire for the knowledge of God's word should supersede all other desires, ambitions, goals and agendas; we should want the life changing word to work in us to the satisfaction of our savior and Lord.

The Lord gave specific instructions to Moses about the children of Israel teaching His word to their children so that they would have a healthy perception of the value of God's word.

- **"And these words, which I command thee this day, shall be in thine heart:**
- **7 And thou shalt teach them diligently unto thy children, and shalt talk of them when thou sittest in thine house, and when thou walkest by the way, and when thou liest**

down, and when thou risest up." (Deut 6:6-7 KJV)
- "Therefore shall ye lay up these my words in your heart and in your soul, and bind them for a sign upon your hand, that they may be as frontlets between your eyes.
- 19 And ye shall teach them your children, speaking of them when thou sittest in thine house, and when thou walkest by the way, when thou liest down, and when thou risest up.
- 20 And thou shalt write them upon the door posts of thine house, and upon thy gates:
- 21 That your days may be multiplied, and the days of your children, in the land which the LORD sware unto your fathers to give them, as the days of heaven upon the earth.
- 22 For if ye shall diligently keep all these commandments which I command you, to do them, to love the LORD your God, to walk in all his ways, and to cleave unto him;
- 23 Then will the LORD drive out all these nations from before you, and ye shall pos-

sess greater nations and mightier than yourselves." (Deut 11:18-23 KJV)

Today's believers talk often about getting back what the enemy has stolen What we need to talk about is getting God's word in our hearts, because that is what it takes to regain our losses and to put the enemy to flight.

Just as the Devil was put in his place by the words that Jesus spoke, we have that same word at our disposal. We just need to make application of that word by speaking it in faith, and the Lord will take it from there. The Word of God is the Word of God and it remains the Word of God. The speaker of that word does not diminish the power of God's living word, and the thing which often prevents the word from manifesting itself is lack of faith.

The truth that Jesus spoke to the man that brought his son for healing is the same truth. He is speaking to us today. **"Jesus said unto him, If thou canst believe, all things are possible to him that believeth." (Mark 9:23 KJV)**

The Lord doesn't need us to make His word true. He needs our faith to activate that true word so that the things offered would apply to our daily lives. His word is true, even if we don't believe it. However, when we believe it, it then comes alive in our favor.

As we practice reading and meditating on the Word of God, that is how we get faith in our spirits. To release that faith we must speak or act upon God's truth.

We tend to want Bible results but fail to speak Biblical truth. It is truth that makes the difference, or should I say that God's word must be faithfully spoken in order to get Bible results.

- **"The prophet that hath a dream, let him tell a dream; and he that hath my word, let him speak my word faithfully. What is the chaff to the wheat? saith the LORD.**
- **29 Is not my word like as a fire? saith the LORD; and like a hammer that breaketh the rock in pieces?" (Jer 23:28-29 KJV)**

No matter what the situation or condition, the answer is the same God's word must be faithfully declared in order to cause a change.

The reason I can say that there is a shortage when it comes to speaking God's word; the Lord says that

His word is **"like a hammer that breaketh the rock in pieces."**

We can tell from the lack of brokenness that the hammer is not striking the designed end. If I am reading correctly, brokenness is the result of being struck by the hammer of God's word. If there is no brokenness, we could conclude that there has been no striking with the hammer or the Word of God has not been faithfully spoken.

I am fully persuaded that nothing short of God's word offers the necessary ingredients to bring about change. That word must be faithfully administered by a faith-filled person whose desire is to please the Lord more than anyone else.

To faithfully deliver the Word of God, a person must truly believe the Word of God and must be persuaded that God and His word are inseparable and unchanging. The conviction and devotion to the word are the very foundation that one must have to faithfully speak God's word without fear of favor. Such a person would be armed and dangerous when it comes to the works of the Devil The enemy would have to regroup time and time again, because he is no match for the Word of God and the believing soul that faithfully employs God's word.

Today's generation is often tempted to go after the techniques of today. They pursue things that sound and appear more pleasant to the eyes and more acceptable by the majority, but they come up empty when it comes to true values and substance. We can be sure that there is nothing this side of heaven that can substitute for the Word of God or that can take the place of God's eternal word. We know that times and things will change but God's word is forever settled in heaven; therefore, it will not change.

The best thing that could happen to any believer is to get hooked on the Word of God and hide it in his or her heart, to do so is to guarantee one's safety. We can't afford to allow the styles and fads of the age to distract our attention.

Let us conclude that God's word is the foundation for our verbal speech and our faith to live by; therefore, let us spend ample time in the word and learn to speak God's word faithfully. God is our greatest example when it comes to speaking those things which be not as if they were; since speaking is one of the ways to release your faith, we need to load our minds, spirits, soul and mouth with God's word and speak faith-filled words with confidence and boldness.

GOD'S WORD IS THE KEY TO OUR POSITIVE CONVERSATION

- **"Thy word have I hid in mine heart, that I might not sin against thee." (Ps 119:11 KJV)**

The Psalmist echoed the need for the word in the heart. He tells what it does for the safety of an individual, and it will keep him or her from sinning against God.

The foundation of our conversation should be the Word of God. When we speak in agreement with God's word, we are sure to be successful in turning away the enemy.

It is the responsibility of every believer to get the Word of God in his or her heart. The word is the only plan that offers guaranteed protection twenty- four seven.

One of the things that make God Word so valuable in these dark and evil days is that it is full of light and the world is flooded with darkness. Not all of that darkness is relegated to the sin-loving world. There is much darkness residing in the lives of believers. Without the light of God's word, we would succumb to the same indwelling darkness that has blinded the world.

When our hearts are flooded with the light of God's word, there is no reason for our stumbling or falling into sin and shame or giving in to the enemy.

"Thy word is a lamp unto my feet, and a light unto my path."(Ps 119:105 KJV)

With the word shining upon our path, we are able to see where we are going. We would never walk in darkness if we would allow God's word to shine in our hearts.

The word of God puts an end to all controversy because it is already settled in heaven. It will never change and neither will God allow it to be defeated.

God's word brings change into one's life and it increases one's level of wisdom and understanding. When we give God's word its rightful place, and we are enhanced in the knowledge of the things of God.

- **"The entrance of thy words giveth light; it giveth understanding unto the simple." (Ps 119:130 KJV)**

We can feel safe in taking a stand on God's word because He keeps watch over His word. He is obligated to fulfill His word, and we can bank on that.

- **"Then said the LORD unto me, Thou hast well seen: for I will hasten my word to perform it." (Jer 1:12 KJV)**
- **"Then said Jehovah unto me, Thou hast well seen: for I watch over my word to perform it" (Jer 1:12 ASV)**
- **"Then the LORD said to me, "You have seen well, for I am watching over My word to perform it." (Jer 1:12 NAS)**

- **"The LORD said to me, "You have seen correctly, for I am watching to see that my word is fulfilled." (Jer 1:12 (from NIV)**

Our God is extremely watchful of the carrying out of His word. He does not utter things which He is unable to bring to pass. He is always in full support of the words that His mouth utters.

- **"So shall my word be that goeth forth out of my mouth: it shall not return unto me void, but it shall accomplish that which I please, and it shall prosper in the thing whereto I sent it" (Isa 55:11 KJV)**

It stands to reason that Jesus lifted up the written Word of God in the face of His enemy. He didn't try to convince the Devil that He was the son of God; He just told him what was written. Now if that was good enough for Jesus, it should be good enough for everyone else.

Jesus reinforces the authority of God's word by using it on the enemy. He reveals to us that the Word of God is all one needs when he or she is facing the enemy. God's word is settled and no one is allowed to change it, He would permit heaven and earth to pass away before the Lord would allow it to fail.

- **"Heaven and earth shall pass away, but my words shall not pass away." (Matt 24:35 KJV)**

We can see why Jesus faithfully repeated, "It is written." He knew that the word would stand regardless of the enemy's threats. He knew that the Devil would have to line up with the Word and behave accordingly.

It is what the Apostle Paul called the sword of the Spirit, which is the Word of God. When a believer speaks what is written he or she has heavens full support in seeing that the Word of God is carried out.

Jesus did not speak His opinion, He chose to use what was written. In other words, He relied on the Word of God that was already written and settled in heaven.

- **"And the devil said unto him, If thou be the Son of God, command this stone that it be made bread.**

- **4 And Jesus answered him, saying, It is written, That man shall not live by bread alone, but by every Word of God." (Luke 4:3-4 KJV)**
- **"If thou therefore wilt worship me, all shall be thine.**
- **8 And Jesus answered and said unto him, Get thee behind me, Satan: for it is written, Thou shalt worship the Lord thy God, and him only shalt thou serve." (Luke 4:7-8 KJV)**
- **"For it is written, He shall give his angels charge over thee, to keep thee:**
- **11 And in their hands they shall bear thee up, lest at any time thou dash thy foot against a stone." (Luke 4:10-11 KJV)**
- **12 And Jesus answering said unto him, It is said, Thou shalt not tempt the Lord thy God." ((Luke 4:12 KJV)**

Satan decided he would use what was written, but he did like many are doing today. He took it out of context and tried to use it to his advantage; however, Jesus was spiritual enough to know the difference and how to rightly divide the Word of God. It would serve us well to take a page out of the Master's book when it comes to defending ourselves with the Word of God. We must not allow the enemy to twist the scriptures and blind our minds to what is written and how it should be applied. We must do like Jesus, we must stay with the written Word of God.

In the Word of God we are safe. Outside the word, we are in serious trouble because the Lord is not obligated to defend that which He has not approved.

- **"And take the helmet of salvation, and the sword of the Spirit, which is the Word of God:" (Eph 6:17 KJV)**

We not only need God's word when we launch an attack against the enemy, but we need the word to perform surgery on our hearts, minds and spirits. The mind is where the enemy seeks to set up his strong holds. We need the Word of God to tear down every strong hold and every evil imagination.

When we are attacked from within and without, we need to rely on the Word of God because it is our best defense against all enemies. We need to learn to speak God's word with faith and courage. We should boldly speak it because it is reliable and already settled in heaven.

- **"(For the weapons of our warfare are not carnal, but mighty through God to the pulling down of strong holds; 2 Corinthians 10:4 KJV)**

THE WAY TO LIFE AND GOOD DAYS

The Bible is the major book that is known to offer a plan that promotes life and good days; however, its instructions often go unheeded by the masses. Let us listen to what the Word of God says. **"What man is he that desireth life, and loveth many days, that he may see good?" (Ps 34:12 KJV)** I feel that the majority of the human race would rather have life and all that it consists of and would love to have it for a long period of time. We would rather have been better than evil during our period of time spent in this world. To have these things the Word of God gives us the instructions that lead to these benefits.

- **"Keep thy tongue from evil, and thy lips from speaking guile." (Ps 34:13 KJV)**

It is imperative for a believer to take full control over what comes out of his or her mouth, because our words reflect what we have in our hearts according to the words of Jesus.

- **"A good man out of the good treasure of his heart bringeth forth that which is good; and an evil man out of the evil treasure of his heart bringeth forth that which is evil: for of the abundance of the heart his mouth speaketh." (Luke 6:45 KJV)**

There is an old saying, "what's in you is sure to come out." The tongue is the thing that expresses what we have in our hearts. We don't have to second guess what's in a person. We only need to stay around him for a while and what's in him would soon be displayed by what comes out of him mouth.

It is high time that we learn that a better heart would result into better speaking. When we commence to deal with what comes out of our mouth, we need to realize that our heart needs help. We should shift our search for help for the heart. If we would receive correction in the heart, it would result in the correction of the mouth. Many people seem spiritual and appear to have a great love for the Lord but when they are looked upon according to the Word of God, we get altogether a different picture. Let us listen to the Apostle James on that subject: **"If anyone considers himself religious and yet does not keep a tight rein on his tongue, he deceives himself and his religion is worthless." (James 1:26 (from NIV)** The word religious could be translated spiritual.

We have support of the importance of proper use of the tongue in many passages of the Word of God. This valuable subject is amplified in both Old and New Testament because of its importance to our future and daily welfare.

It could be said that when the tongue is out of control that one's whole life is unmanageable or is at risk.

- **"He that keepeth his mouth keepeth his life: but he that openeth wide his lips shall have destruction." (Prov 13:3 KJV)**

Many of life's blessings commence with the use of right words or faith-filled words; likewise, many of life's tragedies are preceded by wrong words. That is why it is very important for us to have control over the tongue. We can't afford to allow our bodies to serve our tongues, and we would be better served if our tongues would serve our bodies.

When the tongue serves the body it has to take under consideration the outcome of the words that it utters. In other words, talk must be preceded by a thought.

- **"I said, I will take heed to my ways, that I sin not with my tongue: I will keep my mouth with a bridle, while the wicked is before me." (Ps 39:1 KJV)**
- **"In the multitude of words there wanteth not sin: but he that refraineth his lips is wise." (Prov 10:19 KJV)**
- **"Whoso keepeth his mouth and his tongue keepeth his soul from troubles." (Prov 21:23 KJV)**

Mouth control is very important to the outcome of one's life. The person that fails to control his or her mouth would be the same person that would invite unnecessary trouble into his or her affairs.

It is a fact that there is a time to speak and a time to refrain from speaking. The wise person has his or her tongue under control and surely practices that art.

- **"He that hath knowledge spareth his words: and a man of understanding is of an excellent spirit.**
- **28 Even a fool, when he holdeth his peace, is counted wise: and he that shutteth his lips is esteemed a man of understanding." (Prov 17:27-28 KJV)**

We see in the preceding verses that a person that is truly wise knows how to put his or her mouth on a budget. That is to say, that the wise person refuses to talk, just to be talking. The wise has his or her tongue under control, it is so well disciplined that it only says what is necessary. The controlled tongue is not known for using excessive words to make itself look good or look wise. The text concludes that quietness could be esteemed as understanding. In other words, one could maintain silence and no one would know, one way or the other, what level of understanding he or she had.

When we consider the fact that we have two ears but only one mouth, it is possible that we should do more listening than we do talking. I do know that when one is talking, when he or she should be listening, he or she is sure to miss out on what is being said and when the time comes that the information that was given is called for, that person that was talking more than likely won't have it.

We have viewed some of the Old Testament passages on the use of the tongue. Now let us see what the New Testament has to say on this important matter.

- **"For in many things we offend all. If any man offend not in word, the same is a perfect man, and able also to bridle the whole body." (James 3:2 KJV)**

This is a strong language and a powerful revelation. The man of God concludes that genuine control over one's tongue will qualify one as a mature person in the realm of spirituality. When we use this criterion to measure maturity, I would have to say that we don't have many mature Christians in the church world that I operate in.

That is why the Bible offers a listing of the many sins that are connected to the mouth. Sins of the mouth could be called big mouth sins. I would like to list just a few of the one's that are listed in the Word of God: whispering, backbiting, gossiping, boasting and many others. I may add that these sins that are allowed to operate without many warnings from the modern pulpits. They are called negative words. However, these negative words fuel much fire according to the Word of God.

It should be very difficult for us to read what the Apostle James is saying about the tongue and yet fail to see the need to keep it under control. I feel that we should put forth an even a greater effort to discipline our tongues and train them to serve the body. We should be willing to do whatever is necessary to gain control over our mouth, since we see that it is pregnant with twins. We see that death and life could flow from our own mouth. If you are like me, I want life rather than death. That means I must take control over my tongue.

- **"Behold, we put bits in the horses' mouths, that they may obey us; and we turn about their whole body.**
- **4 Behold also the ships, which though they be so great, and are driven of fierce winds, yet are they turned about with a very small helm, whithersoever the governor listeth." (James 3:3-4 KJV)**

James says we put a bit in the horse's mouth and put a helm on a ship to control them. We need to know that the Lord gave us His Holy Spirit and allowed us to speak in a new language to signify that we are now given a means to discipline the tongue. I am not saying that tongue control takes place overnight, but I am saying that once a person has received the Holy Spirit, he or she is equipped with all the necessary equipment to commence training the tongue. The period of time it takes to train the tongue depends solely on the individual. It would have to do with the desire of the person. If he or she desires to please the Lord more than self, it wouldn't take that person as long as it would be a self-centered person.

One thing we know for sure and that is the mouth would be the chief indicator when it comes to knowing if the person was seeking to please the Lord and seeking a better way and longer and better life.

Now let us return to James's illustration of the horse. You notice that this powerful and fast moving animal is controlled by a small instrument being placed in his mouth. We know that his legs are the things that are in motion or where his great strength is carried out; however, he is controlled by what is placed in his mouth. To omit his mouth is to turn him loose to go as fast as he can and in the direction of his own choice. Likewise, a person that has no control over his or her tongue is sure to go at his or her own pace and in whatever direction, he or she chooses. You take the rudder off a ship and would drift without direction or completely out of control. A person that refuses to discipline his or her mouth is a person that's off course. He or she is sure to make shipwreck of his or her life.

It is true that the instrument that controls the horse and the one the turns the ship are small in comparison to the thing that it controls. The tongue is small, but it carries a very large impact.

If the facts were revealed in many congregations, it would be clear that the tongue was the root cause of many divisions, squabbles, the spreading of wrong information, malicious information, home wrecking, family destroying and other life-destroying conversations. The tongue is known to separate the best of friends, when it engages in loose talk and unfounded words. It is sure to do severe harm to someone.

- **"A froward man soweth strife: and a whisperer separateth chief friends." (Prov 16:28 KJV)**

Just as the bit or the rudder is small in comparison to the horse and the ship the tongue is small in comparison to the body, but it plays a major role when it comes to influencing the life of a person. The tongue is like a spark around a lumberyard or around a California grass field. It could ignite and cause many miles to go up in smoke. A word spoken by an unbridled tongue could set an entire neighborhood aflame with just one word.

- **"Even so the tongue is a little member, and boasteth great things. Behold, how great a matter a little fire kindleth!**
- **6 And the tongue is a fire, a world of iniquity: so is the tongue among our members,**

that it defileth the whole body, and setteth on fire the course of nature; and it is set on fire of hell." (James 3:5-6 KJV)

The tongue could ignite a strong disturbance and an agitation that may be in comparison to world war two or other conflicts it could be done by one sparks from the tongue.

I would feel remiss in neglect sharing with you my Dear Reader the following comments taken from the 6 verse of James. I feel that these words would highlight what I am trying to communicate to you.

- **"A world of iniquity] A little world of evil in itself." This is a very expressive phrase, and is similar to one which we often employ, as when we speak of a town as being a world in miniature. We mean by it that it is an epitome of the world; that all that there is in the world is represented there on a small scale. So when the tongue is spoken of as being "a world of iniquity," it is meant that all kinds of evil that are in the world are exhibited there in miniature; it seems to concentrate all sorts of iniquity that exist** on the earth. And what evil is there, which may not be originated or fomented by the tongue? What else is there that might, with so much propriety, be represented as a little world of iniquity? With all the good which it does, who can estimate the amount of evil which it causes? Who can measure the evils which arise from scandal, and slander, and profaneness, and perjury, and falsehood, and blasphemy, and obscenity, and the inculcation of error, by the tongue? Who can gauge the amount of broils, and contentions, and strife's, and wars, and suspicions, and enmities, and alienations among friends and neighbors, which it produces? Who can number the evils produced by the "honeyed" words of the seducer? or by the tongue of the eloquent in the maintenance of error, and the defense of wrong? If all men were dumb, what a portion of the crimes of the world would soon cease! If all men would speak only that which ought to be spoken, what a change would come over the face of human affairs!" (from Barnes'

Notes, Electronic Database. Copyright (c) 1997 by Biblesoft)

It is time that every believer takes full responsibility for what comes out of his or her mouth, we should stop blaming others for what we do and say. Our tongues would never speak the wrong thing if we were totally void of wrong. Since evil is in our nature, we must train our bodies to obey the leadership of the Spirit of God.

When we learn to be quiet and say the things that make for peace and edify one another, we would then be mature followers of the Lord Jesus Christ.

- *"He that keepeth his mouth keepeth his life: but he that openeth wide his lips shall have destruction." (Prov 13:3 KJV)*
- *"In the multitude of words there wanteth not sin: but he that refraineth his lips is wise." (Prov 10:19 KJV)*
- *"Whoso keepeth his mouth and his tongue keepeth his soul from troubles." (Prov 21:23 KJV)*

If controlling the tongue wasn't highly important, I am sure we wouldn't have so many warnings concerning the use and possibility of abuse. These warnings come to aid us in knowing that the tongue plays a major role in our daily lives. However, the tongue is like a loaded gun, if aimed in the wrong direction, it could cause great harm to some innocent victim. That is why we must seek the face of God and enquire into His help in keeping our tongue on course. We should want our tongues to be used according to its creative purpose.

If we should pray for the Lord's help, we wouldn't be the first to do so, and I trust that we wouldn't be the last because tongue control is much needed.

- **"Set a watch, O LORD, before my mouth; keep the door of my lips."(Ps 141:3 KJV)**

The writer seems to know what the tongue is capable of doing and the risk one runs when the tongue is not under the watchful eye of God. The desire of every believer should be to have his or her tongue used according to divine purpose. When the tongue is used according to God's plan, we could be sure that it would bring glory and honor to His name.

WATCH WHAT YOU SAY

This may seem like a very simple warning. According to the truth found in the Bible, this is a very sober warning that should be heeded by every human being and especially one that believes.

The Word of God is loaded with examples of the misuse of the tongue. We can be sure that we are not immune to the same thing happening to us.

The Bible reveals that the negative use of the tongue could rob and paralyze a whole nation. We see this very thing happening to ancient Israel through the mouth of the men that went to spy out the land that the Lord had given them.

They gave a good report of what was in the land. This report included everything that was there even the people that dwelled in the land, but they took it too far by putting more stress on the opposition than they did the benefits.

- "So they went up, and searched the land from the wilderness of Zin unto Rehob, as men come to Hamath.
- 22 And they ascended by the south, and came unto Hebron; where Ahiman, Sheshai, and Talmai, the children of Anak, were. (Now Hebron was built seven years before Zoan in Egypt.)
- 23 And they came unto the brook of Eshcol, and cut down from thence a branch with one cluster of grapes, and they bare it between two upon a staff; and they brought of the pomegranates, and of the figs.
- 24 The place was called the brook Eshcol, because of the cluster of grapes which the children of Israel cut down from thence.
- 25 And they returned from searching of the land after forty days." (Num 13:21-25 KJV)

When you examine the report that the spies gave you would find that it was a true report. To authenticate their report, they brought back samples of what was found in the land. Their report and samples were all that was needed because the Lord had already said that He had given them the land. Keep in mind that these men were ordered to go and search out the land, but they were also supposed to check it for its fruitfulness. They were to find out if it was just as the Lord had told them.

It is true that they were supposed to check out the people in the land; however, I don't think the Lord wanted them to put more emphasis on the opposition than they did the fruitfulness of the land.

You could be sure that over emphasizing or stressing the well being of the opposition won't bring victory. We must stress what the Lord says and take our stand on His word.

- **"Send thou men, that they may search the land of Canaan, which I give unto the children of Israel: of every tribe of their fathers shall ye send a man, every one a ruler among them." (Num 13:2 KJV)**
- **"And Moses sent them to spy out the land of Canaan, and said unto them, Get you**

up this way southward, and go up into the mountain:
- **18 And see the land, what it is; and the people that dwelleth therein, whether they be strong or weak, few or many;**
- **19 And what the land is that they dwell in, whether it be good or bad; and what cities they be that they dwell in, whether in tents, or in strong holds;**
- **20 And what the land is, whether it be fat or lean, whether there be wood therein, or not. And be ye of good courage, and bring of the fruit of the land. Now the time was the time of the firstripe grapes." (Num 13:17-20 KJV)**

The confidence they needed should have been found in the fact that the Lord said that He had given the land to His people that is the thing that mattered most. They had been up against difficulties before and had faced many enemies, yet came out victorious because the Lord was their source. He was willing to lead them all the way.

There has been no change in the principle of the Lord being there to help His people when they face great odds. This is yet His order. This is especially true when the people of God put full trust in His word.

- **"And they told him, and said, We came unto the land whither thou sentest us, and surely it floweth with milk and honey; and this is the fruit of it.**
- **28 Nevertheless the people be strong that dwell in the land, and the cities are walled, and very great: and moreover we saw the children of Anak there.**
- **29 The Amalekites dwell in the land of the south: and the Hittites, and the Jebusites, and the Amorites, dwell in the mountains: and the Canaanites dwell by the sea, and by the coast of Jordan." (Num 13:27-29 KJV)**

To read the report given by the spies, one must wonder had they forgotten that the Lord had given them the land, and that He was in their midst to fight their battles. How could they allow the opposition to influence them more than the promises of God? I ask knowing fully that human nature has many defects and one of them is fear. The people that they saw were more real to them than God's promise. In fact, the size of the people and security of their cities were intimidating enough to paralyze their desire to obtain the land.

Before we commence to criticize ancient Israel, we should examine ourselves and make sure that we are in full compliance with God's promises to us. One thing we should learn from this scenario is the danger of the tongue. The people that spoke influenced the ones that were not there to see what they had seen, but they made what they had seen so real the others felt what they were saying and acted accordingly.

The spies that went to check out the land were made afraid by what they saw. They returned and filled the others with their fear. Fear comes the same way faith does and that is by hearing. When the people heard what the fearful said, it made them afraid. They grew afraid of what they hadn't seen from the words of the ones that had viewed the situation.

The thing that made this fear so devastating was that it was spoken. They were not willing to keep it to themselves, and they wanted everyone to know what they had seen and how they felt about what they saw.

- **"But the men that went up with him said, We be not able to go up against the people; for they are stronger than we.**
- **32 And they brought up an evil report of the land which they had searched unto the children of Israel, saying, The land, through which we have gone to search it, is a land that eateth up the inhabitants thereof; and all the people that we saw in it are men of a great stature.**
- **33 And there we saw the giants, the sons of Anak, which come of the giants: and we were in our own sight as grasshoppers, and so we were in their sight." (Num 13:31-33 KJV)**

The report given by the spies is a typical example of what a negative tongue can do. It didn't just affect the one or ones that were speaking, but their negative tongue influenced the whole congregation with few exceptions.

The fear reporters declared that they were not able to go up against the people of the land. They saw their opposition as stronger than they were. The real problem was the fact that they failed to include

God in this matter,. It was the Lord that had given them the land, and He knew exactly the condition of the land from day one.

Their report was called an evil report. It was evil because it emphasized the problem while overlooking the provision and the answer. Human nature is good at making the problem larger than the answer. That is the thing that opens the door for failure and defeat. In reality, there is no problem that is bigger than our God, neither is anything too hard for Him. He is more than equal to every task His children face.

The mouth of the majority was filled with fear-filled words. They were in full support of the opposition and didn't know that anytime anyone speaks fear filled words he or she is supporting the opposition. Let us notice their words: *"We be not able to go up against the people; for they are stronger than we."* These are defeating words. It is the language that prevents one from even trying to succeed. They were DOA (dead on arrival). They were looking through the eyes of fear. The impact of fear is known to stop one in his or her track. In other words, fear causes defeat without effort.

Again their report was called an evil report, because it put the enemy in control without a possibility of being defeated. **"The land, through which we have gone to search it, is a land that eateth up the inhabitants thereof; and all the people that we saw in it are men of a great stature."**

The spies sounded as if they had first hand knowledge of the people's strength and ability to fight. They failed to focus on the one that had given them the land. Their attitude reminds me of believers testifying, but giving the credit to the enemy by saying what he is doing and how hard things are and how much trouble they are facing. That kind of speech strengthens the grip of the enemy that allows him to hold one captive without putting forth any effort. A person thinking or talking along those lines is helping the enemy. To strengthen their claim, they gave this description of the opposition: **"And there we saw the giants, the sons of Anak, which come of the giants: and we were in our own sight as grasshoppers, and so we were in their sight."**

It is too bad that they could see the giants but failed to remember the greatness of their God. They were following the same One that had dried up the Red Sea right before their eyes. There were many other miracles He had performed. When one is busy focusing on the problem, it is easy to overlook the answer. They saw how large the opposition was, but failed to see the largeness of their God.

It would be wise for us to learn a lesson from ancient Israel and not to make a similar mistake by focusing on our problems while totally overlooking our answer. And let us not spend more time describing our situation, problem and opposition than we spend describing the largeness, greatness, faithfulness and love of our Lord.

From some sources, the description that was given of the Anakites was exaggerated. There is no reason to doubt that the people in that land were rugged looking men, but to stand so tall that it made others seem as small as grasshoppers is a bit much. You know and I know that fear paints a picture different from normal. It sees what no one else can see because the problem is on the inside.

Remember, fear does for the enemy what faith does for God. The Bible tells us that faith cometh by hearing and so does fear. They both have the potential to impact one's life. That is why it is so important for us to fill our mouth with faith-filled words, so that we can impact lives for good and to the glory of God.

Just as faith carries the power and influence to move people toward God, its counterpart fear, moves people away from the Lord and fills them with Satan's thoughts. The men that gave an evil report were so persuasive that they were able to influence the majority. They inflicted the congregation with much unnecessary hardship, agony and anger. They put the people in such a state of weeping and crying, that I conclude as unnecessary because the Lord was willing and able to give them the land and defeat the enemies regardless of their size.

- **"And all the congregation lifted up their voice, and cried; and the people wept that night.**
- **2 And all the children of Israel murmured against Moses and against Aaron: and the whole congregation said unto them, Would God that we had died in the land of Egypt! or would God we had died in this wilderness!**
- **3 And wherefore hath the LORD brought us unto this land, to fall by the sword, that our wives and our children should be a**

prey? were it not better for us to return into Egypt?" (Num 14:1-3 KJV)

The fear driven spies did what all scared people do, they spread their fears among the congregation to the degree the people started crying as if they had no one to help them. They completely forgot that the Lord was with them, and that He had promised to give them the land. The text said: **"and the people wept that night."** I say that they spent a night wasting energy because they were under the influence of negative thinking and talking people. People that are driven by fear are subject to say things that are very drastic. They are known to talk out of their heads because their motivation is founded in fear. **"Would God that we had died in the land of Egypt! or would God, we had died in this wilderness!"** They were completely void of gratitude for the blessings that they had already received and for the promise the Lord had made them. They were persuaded that were unable to go forth into the land because of the opposition. It is common when one is unwilling to go forth his or her mind turns back to what is familiar or to what seems easiest to deal with. Fear made them think about returning to Egypt. They spoke as if their lives in slavery were more beneficial than following the ways of the Lord.

They then put their foot in their mouth by accusing the Lord of bringing them out into the wilderness to die by the sword. "**And wherefore hath the LORD brought us unto this land, to fall by the sword.**" Fear is known to make one play the blame game. When one becomes so fearful that he or she directs his or her blame toward the Lord, that is what I call going too far.

I think that we often overlook the fact that if the Lord wanted us dead it wouldn't take someone else to do it for Him. He could just say the word, and we would be gone. It would be good if we would remember that fact when sickness strikes our bodies. We should focus on the fact that the Lord trying to kill us, because He doesn't need to make us sick in order to kill us. All He has to do is withhold the next breath, and we would be out of here.

- **"Thou hidest thy face, they are troubled: thou takest away their breath, they die, and return to their dust." (Ps 104:29 KJV)**

I do not believe that the Lord would kill or let anyone die that is trying to fulfill His will before the job is finished; however, I do believe that the enemy would love to see us dead before we could complete the Lord's will for our lives. That is why the enemy tries to flood our hearts and minds with fear so that we would accuse the Lord of trying to kill us. Allow me to say again, if the Lord wanted us dead there is no medicine or doctor that could prevent us from dying. We should feel that every morning that our eyes open, it is a sign that the Lord wants us to live.

It was too bad that Israel didn't know that the Lord wanted them to possess the land. He knew that the so-called giants were there. He never withholds his blessing and promises just because problems seem gigantic or insurmountable, He is well able to fulfill His word.

We can be sure that the enemy is capable of making things seem too large or too tough for us in hopes of us becoming afraid and wanting to turn back. We need to remind ourselves that the Lord is our source and whatever He delights in doing for us no one or nothing can stop Him.

Now that we have spent time to consider the ones that spoke in support of the enemy, we should now take a look at the one's that spoke in favor of the will of God.

First of all, we should thank the Lord that He never leaves Himself without a witness. It matters not what the circumstances are, there will always be someone that is willing to stand on God's word. We find two out of the twelve that saw things through the eyes of faith. They didn't hesitate to express their willingness to go up and possess the land.

- **"Then Caleb silenced the people before Moses and said, "We should go up and take possession of the land, for we can certainly do it." (from NIV)**

Faith does not hide itself when it is in an atmosphere embalmed with fear. It will speak what it believes because faith knows that the Lord will make good His promises.

By the time the negative majority thinks that faith has been silenced, it will speak repeatedly until the Word of God has been declared. Faith-filled words are known to foster life. It is also known to keep one inspired until the will of the Lord is fulfilled in his or her life.

It is a fact that what is in a person is sure to come out. The negative majority had no problem proclaiming their fears and neither did the faith-filled minority have a problem speaking faith-filled words.

The faith-filled representatives of the Lord didn't let the majority sway them in believing that they were better off in Egypt. They knew that the Lord had provided for them a much better place than Egypt.

While the fear-stricken majority called for the formulation of a back to Egypt's committee, the true servants of God had no interest in going backward they wanted to go forward and possess what was theirs.

We should learn from Israel's reaction and Joshua and Caleb's stance that its best to speak for God than to be influenced by those speaking on behalf of the enemies of God.

- **"And they said one to another, Let us make a captain, and let us return into Egypt.**

- 5 Then Moses and Aaron fell on their faces before all the assembly of the congregation of the children of Israel." (Num 14:4-5 KJV)

Let us thank the Lord right now that He always has someone that is willing to use his or her mouth to represent Him. The masses may try to drown the voice of God's spokesperson, but faith will not give in to fear.

"And Joshua the son of Nun, and Caleb the son of Jephunneh, which were of them that searched the land, rent their clothes:

7 And they spake unto all the company of the children of Israel, saying, The land, which we passed through to search it, is an exceeding good land.

8 If the LORD delight in us, then he will bring us into this land, and give it us; a land which floweth with milk and honey.

9 Only rebel not ye against the LORD, neither fear ye the people of the land; for they are bread for us: their defence is departed

from them, and the LORD is with us: fear them not." (Num 14:6-9 KJV)

It should be encouraging to our faith to know that when Joshua and Caleb went with the group, more than likely they saw what the others saw but their assessment was completely different from the majority.

When one views things through the eyes of faith, that person sees things from God's view point. I am not saying that faith is blind, it is not blind. It just has a better and clearer view because faith has the eyes of God to see through.

Joshua and Caleb believed God before they made the trip; therefore, nothing they saw changed their minds about what the Lord had promised. They were persuaded that God had given them the land, and that they had nothing to do but go over and possess it.

They pleaded with the congregation to not rebel against the Lord, neither fear the people because the people would be defenseless against them since the Lord had given them the land.

Joshua and Caleb did exactly what faith-filled people do they rejected the voice of fear by declaring that their God was able to give them the land. Joshua and Caleb refused to aid the opposition by describing their seemingly advantages, they were too focused on the largeness of their God.

The church of today needs more Joshuas and Calebs; we need spokespersons that can see beyond the smoke screen of fear, doubt, unbelief, intimidation and worldly darkness. We need men and women that are willing to open their mouth and speak in favor of God's greatness and faithfulness. We need voices to amplify the good things of the Lord so that those that are without would desire to know our God.

Let's face it, our words carry influence. We should consider that before we open our mouth. We should think that someone is sure to be affected by the things we say. That is why we should speak words that would better a person's condition and not leave them worse than we found them.

DON'T JUST LISTEN YOU NEED TO TALK

When the Bible says that faith cometh by hearing, that statement includes the hearing of the things that the Lord has done. We should learn to speak in agreement with what is written.

We saw in the previous chapter that Joshua and Caleb didn't allow the fearful ones to speak for them. They stepped up and declared that the God that they served was well able to give them what He had promised.

They didn't let fear drown their voices. All believers must stay on guard against the intimidation of fear that would try to silence the voice of faith. We must believe what we accept as the will of God so strongly that nothing or nobody could conquer our conviction.

Fear is known to make things appear so large that it clouds one's vision of God. That is why the enemy speaks so loudly, he wants his voice only to be heard. When we hear the voice of fear only, we stand little to no chance of overcoming our situation. That is why our ears must hear our mouth speak the things that awaken faith in our hearts.

- Let me once again refer to Caleb and how he spoke at the peak of a fearful conversation: **"And Caleb stilled the people before Moses, and said, Let us go up at once, and possess it; for we are well able to overcome it." (Num 13:30 KJV)**

People of faith have more right to speak than those driven by fear, because they represent the God of faith, and He is working for the good of His people.

When I say that one needs to talk, his or her talk is not limited to his or her mouth. This also includes one's actions. It was said of Noah that he is yet speaking, not with his voice but with his life, by the things he did in a negative environment. Noah was so busy doing the will of the Lord that he didn't have time to play. His generation was so busy playing that they didn't have time to build. It is much like that in my day, the sin-loving world is so busy playing that they don't have time to live holy. However, the people of faith must maintain a life of consistency before the Lord until He comes. We must speak loud by the lives that we live. We cannot settle for the here and now, we must be persuaded that there is a hereafter that we must prepare for while we are here in this evil world.

We should learn from the examples in the Scriptures that speaking unlocks the hidden treasures in a person and equips them with courage to go forth for the Lord.

The method of speaking faith and courage into one's life can be seen when the Lord spoke into Gideon's life. The Lord did not call him according to his actions but spoke past his fears to his faith.

- **"And there came an angel of the LORD, and sat under an oak which was in Ophrah, that pertained unto Joash the Abi-ezrite:**

> and his son Gideon threshed wheat by the winepress, to hide it from the Midianites.
> - 12 And the angel of the LORD appeared unto him, and said unto him, The LORD is with thee, thou mighty man of valour' 9 Judg 6:12 KJV)

According to Gideon's actions, he was afraid but the Lord didn't call him a chicken, He called him a mighty man of valour.

Faith-filled words are designed to wake up that part of us that the Lord can use, He has no room for fear. He is seeking men and women that are willing to walk by faith.

The assignment that the Lord had for Gideon took genuine faith. That is why the Lord hailed him as a mighty man of valour. He called him according to what He saw in Gideon. That was the divine way of waking up the warrior that resided in this man of faith. He needed to hear God's assessment of him.

When the Lord speaks to us, we are then able to speak to surrounding conditions because hearing from the Master floods the heart with faith and courage.

The task that Gideon was called upon to carry out was a gigantic one nothing and less than faith could qualify him for the job.

The life of Gideon speaks volumes of faith and courage. His life story should light a fire under ever one that reads it. Here is a man that took a three hundred- man army and won over multitudes. He didn't allow the size of the opposition to hide his view of the true and living God.

> **"And the Midianites and the Amalekites and all the children of the east lay along in the valley like grasshoppers for multitude; and their camels were without number, as the sand by the sea side for multitude." (Judg 7:12 KJV)**

If my calculation is correct Gideon and his three hundred-man army had to overcome combined nations of armies; nevertheless, they came out winners because their trust was in the Lord of Lords.

Faith doesn't have to have majority support in order for it to work. Faith is known to work in spite of circumstances. When all odds seem against a person of faith, that is when faith stands the tallest and makes its voice to be heard the clearest.

Isaac did plant his crops because he saw the season was favorable. He planted because he believed that God would prosper from the work of his hands. It is common knowledge that sowing during a famine would be more like wasting your seeds, but when a thing is done in faith it gives the Lord something to work with.

> **"Then Isaac sowed in that land, and received in the same year an hundredfold: and the LORD blessed him." (Gen 26:12 KJV)**

The famine didn't prevent Isaac from being blessed. It was severe enough to put the crops of others on hold but the man of faith demonstrated what his God could do in the face of great odds. When the blessing of the Lord is upon someone, conditions don't have to be favorable, the Lord has His own way of bringing things to pass.

Based upon the words written concerning Abel, a person's actions speaks even after they are gone into eternity. That is why we have so many accounts of faith left in the Bible. I would love to join in with the heroes of the Bible by living a life of faith and leave behind the kind of example that would inspire faith in others.

> **"By faith Abel offered unto God a more excellent sacrifice than Cain, by which he obtained witness that he was righteous, God testifying of his gifts: and by it he being dead yet speaketh." (Heb 11:4 KJV)**

Just as we have lives in the Bible that spoke by their action, we also have examples of speaking to life's challenges and opposition.

King David has been hailed as one who spoke to the opposition with courage and boldness by the name of the Lord God of Israel. His experience with the Lord fueled his faith to meet the challenge.

David was truly challenged by a giant; however, he never once called him a giant instead David called him an uncircumcised Gentile. He didn't support the efforts of the enemy by suggesting that he had an advantage.

We should have learned from ancient Israel not to support the efforts of the enemy by making the problem bigger than the answer. Our focus should always be on the greatness of our God and His willingness to bless us with what we have need in spite of the myriad of opposition.

When our relationships are anchored in the Lord, we are bold in our speech toward testing conditions. We are not easily intimidated or turned aside, and we are able to maintain that feeling that everything is going to be all right.

David is a typical example that trouble is sure to find you wherever you are. It was his experience with the Lion and Bear that gave him courage to face the giant.

Moving from one experience to another is God way of promotion, the Lord takes us from level one to a higher level and each one comes with a different experience.

David didn't go to the battlefield to fight, he went to check on his brothers. He just happened to be to hear and see what was going on. What he heard caused the God in him to be stirred to action.

It is difficult for a person of faith to maintain silence when the enemy is making unfounded threats and using the name of the King of glory in vain.

"And David left his carriage in the hand of the keeper of the carriage, and ran into the army, and came and saluted his brethren.

23 And as he talked with them, behold, there came up the champion, the Philistine of Gath, Goliath by name, out of the armies of the Philistines, and spake according to the same words: and David heard them.

24 And all the men of Israel, when they saw the man, fled from him, and were sore afraid.

25 And the men of Israel said, Have ye seen this man that is come up? surely to defy Israel is he come up: and it shall be, that the man who killeth him, the king will enrich him with great riches, and will give him his daughter, and make his father's house free in Israel.

26 And David spake to the men that stood by him, saying, What shall be done to the man that killeth this Philistine, and taketh away the reproach from Israel? for who is this uncircumcised Philistine, that he should defy the armies of the living God?

27 And the people answered him after this manner, saying, So shall it be done to the

man that killeth him." (1 Sam 17:22-27 KJV)

Until David arrived on the scene, Goliath had conquered the armies of Israel using his mouth. He used intimidation to corner his enemies. They credited him with the ability to do what he said. No man was willing to challenge him. They made him the champion without a fight.

We saw fear disturb ancient Israel and made them want to go back into slavery rather than possess the land that the Lord had given them.

David arrived on the scene in time to hear Goliath bellow out his threats. It appears that he used the same speech daily, but this time a person of faith was on the scene. People of faith are not easily intimidated by empty threats.

King Saul too was afraid. That is why he offered a reward to the person that was willing to fight against the enemy and overcome him.

The reward was rehearsed in the ears of David. He responded with courage because he felt that the big fellow had overstepped his bounds by defying the armies of the living God.

It is always an extra blessing when a person of faith is in the midst. He or she is known to change the entire atmosphere when he or she speaks. Just as Caleb stilled the people before Moses, now we have David ready to represent the true and living God by putting an end to that negative talk of the opposition. The bold faith of David came with a "put up or shut up" approach because he knew that the Lord was with him.

- **"And when the words were heard which David spake, they rehearsed them before Saul: and he sent for him.**
- **32 And David said to Saul, Let no man's heart fail because of him; thy servant will go and fight with this Philistine." (1 Sam 17:31-32 KJV)**

David's courage sent a buzz throughout the camp. They even brought the man of faith to King Saul; however, the king tried to shift his fear on to David, but he was prepared to answer all challenges. David spoke words of encouragement to the fear driven king. He didn't want the king or anyone else to spend anymore time fearing because the Lord had sent him to put an end to the threat that they had faced for days.

What we hear coming out of Saul's mouth is the reason we must learn to speak on the Lord's behalf. If we don't, the fearful will keep the enemy in command by supporting him with negative speech and thought.

King Saul was afraid of the challenger. Therefore, he was doing what fearful people do; he was rehearsing his fears to David so that he too would fall in line. However, David was marching by a different drumbeat. He had spent too much time with the Lord to be overcome by fear.

David didn't need Saul to tell him what he couldn't do. He knew that he had help, the Lord was his helper, he wasn't about to listen to what the fearful had to say, he was too busy listening to the Lord. A person of faith draws his or her inspiration from the Lord that he or she loves and honors. That is the thing that drives fear away, one's love for the King of Kings.

Saul was quick to make his comparison between the two; however, he didn't seem to know anything about David and didn't seem to know much about the Lord that David served. That is why we can't afford to allow the people that don't really know the Lord to tell us what the Lord can do. The people of faith are the ones that should do the talking. Because we have experiences with the living God, our knowledge of Him would be helpful for others. It is almost impossible for a person displaying faith not to impact others. This is often done without any suggestion being made. It is because faith is contagious, and it is without a doubt worth catching.

- **"And David said unto Saul, Thy servant kept his father's sheep, and there came a lion, and a bear, and took a lamb out of the flock:**
- **35 And I went out after him, and smote him, and delivered it out of his mouth: and when he arose against me, I caught him by his beard, and smote him, and slew him.**
- **36 Thy servant slew both the lion and the bear: and this uncircumcised Philistine shall be as one of them, seeing he hath defied the armies of the living God.**
- **37 David said moreover, The LORD that delivered me out of the paw of the lion, and out of the paw of the bear, he will deliver**

> **me out of the hand of this Philistine. And Saul said unto David, Go, and the LORD be with thee." (1 Sam 17:34-37 KJV)**

To awaken the faith of the king, David gave him his testimony. He encouraged the king by sharing what the Lord had done in the past. He changed the speech of the king with his experiences, and it led to the king giving his approval. Faith is known to turn things around for the good of all. That is why we must speak faith-filled words at all times, we are sure to help someone and usher in the presence of the living God.

- **"And Saul armed David with his armour, and he put an helmet of brass upon his head; also he armed him with a coat of mail.**
- **39 And David girded his sword upon his armour, and he assayed to go; for he had not proved it. And David said unto Saul, I cannot go with these; for I have not proved them. And David put them off him." (1 Sam 17:38-39 KJV)**

King Saul made another attempt to display his approval by putting his own armour on David; however, David recognized that he had never practiced with that type of equipment. He was willing to stick with what he knew had worked in the past. Another person's testimony won't work for us in our crisis. We need to know for ourselves that the Lord is faithful. We cannot depend on what others are saying, we must know for ourselves.

David quickly detected that Saul's equipment might work for him, but it was not suited for David. When you know that you are outside your ability, there is noting left to do but line up with what you know. That is exactly what David did. We must know ourselves that the Lord is faithful. We cannot depend on what is said by others, we must know for ourselves.

- **"And he took his staff in his hand, and chose him five smooth stones out of the brook, and put them in a shepherd's bag which he had, even in a scrip; and his sling was in his hand: and he drew near to the Philistine."(1Sam 17:40 KJV) for ourselves.**

It would serve well to take note how this young lad armed himself with what he knew, and what he had used before with success. He didn't feel comfortable wearing what might work for someone else. He stayed within his own experience and knowledge.

The church would be better off today if we would practice abiding in our callings and not be lured into trying to do what we see others do. No matter how well someone does a thing, we could be sure that there is something that we could do well. When we discover that which we do well, is our gift from God. We should abide in our anointing.

We should all know this fact. The Lord is under no obligation to support that which is designed by a human effort.

- **"And the Philistine came on and drew near unto David; and the man that bare the shield went before him.**
- **42 And when the Philistine looked about, and saw David, he disdained him: for he was but a youth, and ruddy, and of a fair countenance.**
- **43 And the Philistine said unto David, Am I a dog, that thou comest to me with**

staves? And the Philistine cursed David by his gods.

Goliath's previous success had been achieved by him doing all the talking. However, his talk in the past had been to people that were afraid. He is now facing one that was full of faith and courage and that reduced his talk to no more than empty words.

People of faith don't let the opposition do all the talking because faith-filled people have their own conversation. Their words are backed by a living and powerful God.

A person of faith would feel remiss to remain silent in the face of a fear- promoting situation. David was not intimidated by Goliath's size or sound. He was there to represent the God of Israel, the God and nation that Goliath had defied. It was now time for him to pay.

Another thing we could learn from David, is that we cannot afford to let what the opposition says penetrate our thoughts. We must focus on what we know the Lord is saying to and through us.

We must not let the description that the enemy makes of us cause us to line up with his words. We must know who we are and whose we are at all times.

- **"Then said David to the Philistine, Thou comest to me with a sword, and with a spear, and with a shield: but I come to thee in the name of the LORD of hosts, the God of the armies of Israel, whom thou hast defied.**
- **46 This day will the LORD deliver thee into mine hand; and I will smite thee, and take thine head from thee; and I will give the carcases of the host of the Philistines this day unto the fowls of the air, and to the wild beasts of the earth; that all the earth may know that there is a God in Israel." (1 Sam 17:45-46 KJV)**

David's faith and courage allowed him to cast off the words of the enemy. He knew that his God was with him and that this over-sized, vociferous, trouble-maker was just another day at the office.

To win the war of words, one must know the God of the word as well as the letter of the word. It worked for Jesus and David, it will work for you and me.

When David told him that he had come in the name of the Lord of host, he identified the Lord as the God of Israel, the very nation that this talker had defied.

David then told him that it was his last day. He told him that he would become buzzard bait that same day and that wild beast would have him for supper.

Faith will not allow the opposition to talk without limits, because a person of faith has to act on God's message. A person of faith waits to hear the voice of the Lord to turn on the light of hope. When the light of hope comes on, no challenge is too great to face.

Faith announces to the opposition the exact message his defeat will send to all that are involved and that message is: **"that there is a God in Israel."** Every defeat of an enemy is a reminder that our God is an awesome God.

When we look at 1 Samuel from a historical account, we can better understand why David continually refers to Goliath as "**this uncircumcised Philistine**." This covers the fact that Goliath has no covenant right to the land. Goliath came from a city that should have been utterly destroyed, but was allowed to remain by the leadership of Judah in the book of Judges. Now Gath in the form of Goliath has come back to trouble Israel.

- **"And all this assembly shall know that the LORD saveth not with sword and spear: for the battle is the LORD's, and he will give you into our hands." (1 Sam 17:47 KJV)**

By faith David knew who the battle belonged to. He knew that more was at stake than just fighting with an oversized man. It was show time and time to display God's power over an already defeated enemy. An enemy from a tribe that should have been wiped out much earlier but was allowed to live because of negligence on the part of Judah's past leadership.

David wasn't about to make that same mistake. It was time to put an end to the reign of this strong opposition. It was time to cut him down to size so that everyone could see the hand of God at work.

- **"And it came to pass, when the Philistine arose, and came and drew nigh to meet David, that David hasted, and ran toward the army to meet the Philistine.**

- **49 And David put his hand in his bag, and took thence a stone, and slang it, and smote the Philistine in his forehead, that the stone sunk into his forehead; and he fell upon his face to the earth.**
- **50 So David prevailed over the Philistine with a sling and with a stone, and smote the Philistine, and slew him; but there was no sword in the hand of David.**
- **51 Therefore David ran, and stood upon the Philistine, and took his sword, and drew it out of the sheath thereof, and slew him, and cut off his head therewith. And when the Philistines saw their champion was dead, they fled." (1 Sam 17:48-52 KJV)**

David's faith and courage motivated him to hasten toward the challenger. He knew that the Lord was with him. He was ready to be used by the Lord and bring courage back into the camp of God's people. When Goliath fell to the ground, fear fell with him and boldness stood with David. When faith prevails fear must flee. Just as the followers of Goliath fled when they saw that he was defeated, that is exactly what victory is supposed to do. That is why we need the people of faith to stand up and meet the challenges of today so that others will take faith and stand up with us.

The human race needs to see believer knock down the giants of our age so that they too can catch hold of faith. This world is facing many giant-like situations in ever area of life, home, school, church, work place community, body, mind, and spirit. More defeat is not what we need to see. We need to see the Lord's battle fought in faith and victories won to the glory of His name.

- **"And the men of Israel and of Judah arose, and shouted, and pursued the Philistines, until thou come to the valley, and to the gates of Ekron. And the wounded of the Philistines fell down by the way to Shaaraim, even unto Gath, and unto Ekron." (1 Sam 17:52 KJV)**

When believers slay the giants of unholy living, worldly compromise and spiritual ignorance, we are sure to inspire others to come out of hiding and pursue the enemy with courage. I am persuaded that every victory won carries great sparks of inspiration. Someone is sure to be moved by what he or she sees.

After David slew Goliath the people heard and saw an emotion in the camp that surpassed any they had seen. It was because the real champion was on their side and that gave them reason for rejoicing.

When wrong-living people see the saints of God living a holy and upright life, they will then know that the salvation of Jesus Christ is more than a church thing. They will know that it is obtainable after seeing it practiced before their very eyes.

Victorious living by a representative of the faith would be somewhat like David killing a giant. It will bring into reality what was once looked upon as impossible. The thing that will make living right in this wrong world so outstanding is that we are living in the age of compromise and one of the first things that seems to go out of the window is our strong convictions for holy living.

The church world is flooded with a mimicking spirit. We seem to want to be like what we see. Since everybody else doing it, why shouldn't I? That seems to be the spirit of church world.

It is high time that we take on the spirit of David and tackle this giant of spiritual imitating and stand up for what is right. We need to represent the living God in a manner that others would take courage and stand. We need to follow Noah's example. He was so busy doing the will of God that he didn't have time to play. Although everybody else was playing, he kept building.

I am convinced that the more one involves himself or herself in the will of God the less time he or she would have for the devil and this world. It is a spiritually dangerous thing to be too casual or non-committed to the things of the Lord.

To maintain a healthy and fresh daily demeanor, we need to often speak the right words. We must keep our mouth filled with truth. It is to our advantage to speak often of the Lord's goodness, mercy and longsuffering on our behalf. When our mouth is filled with thanksgiving and praise, we are not likely to use our mouth for evil expressions while we are busy using it for the Lord.

TURNING THINGS AROUND WITH RIGHT WORDS

Our words have power to turn things around, which is why we must watch what we say. Our words can promote happiness as well as sadness. They can promote peace as well as war. The Bible says that the tongue carries death and life.

- **"Death and life are in the power of the tongue: and they that love it shall eat the fruit thereof." (Prov 18:21 KJV)**

The tongue is somewhat like a trigger on a loaded gun. If it is aimed in the wrong directions it could cause tragic harm to some. When we speak without watching our words, we could cause irreparable harm to someone's character.

"Your words, your dreams, and your thoughts have power to create conditions in your life.

What you speak about, you can bring about.

If you keep saying you can't stand your job, you might lose your job.

If you keep saying you can't stand your body, your body can become sick.

If you keep saying you can't stand your car, your car could be stolen or just stop operating.

If you keep saying you're broke, guess what? You'll always be broke.

If you keep saying you can't trust a man or trust a woman, you will always find someone in your life to hurt and betray you.

If you keep saying you can't find a job, you will remain unemployed.

If you keep saying you can't find someone to love you or believe in you, your very thought will attract more experiences to confirm your beliefs.

If you keep talking about a divorce or breakup in a relationship, then you might end up with it.

The Key To Your Future Is In Your Mouth

Turn your thoughts and conversations around to be more positive and power packed with faith, hope, love and action. Don't be afraid to believe that you can have what you want and deserve.

Watch your Thoughts, they become words.
Watch your Words, they become actions.
Watch your Actions, they become habits.
Watch your Habits, they become character.
Watch your Character, for it becomes your Destiny.

Watch how your circumstances and situations begin to change when you change the way you speak. I thought I would share this with you. (Submitted by Pieter van Wyk on the internet on May 26, 2009)

It is common for someone to say when they hear you sneeze, you sound like you are coming down with a fresh cold, and you should say, "I might be going up with something but I am not coming down with anything." We have to be careful how we respond to words spoken by others, because their doubts and fears are subject to influence us.

We need to keep in mind that people who constantly talk doubt are speaking death and those who speak faith-filled words are speaking life. You can be sure that both will get what they say.

Right words carry the potential for healing, inspiration, motivation, encouragement revelation and life. The wise man Solomon said it well when he said: **"A word fitly spoken is like apples of gold in pictures of silver."(Prov 25:11 KJV)**

The word pictures could be translated baskets. **"Fitly spoken"** is a phrase that means timely or appropriate. The only realistic word that I know fits the description of apples of gold is the Bible. Appropriate or timely words could add refreshing to ones life when he or she is struggling with some of life's difficulties. The right word could make the task much easier to bear.

Since the Word of God is so powerful, one could speak the living word to himself or herself and bring joy to himself or herself, because the Word of God contains every answer to my need.

- **"A man hath joy by the answer of his mouth: and a word spoken in due season, how good is it!"(Prov 15:23 KJV)**

The Word of God is good for every season. It always brings joy. It is the answer that every mouth should know and experience.

The Bible supports one encouraging himself. That is exactly what David did when his life was being threatened. This was no doubt one of the low points in his life. First of all he had lost his family and he could see ruins of fire right before his very eyes. To add to all that was going on, his own support group was talking about killing him for what had happened to their families.

David did what every believing and trusting soul must do. He turned his focus to the Lord, the only one that could help him in a time like he was encountering. It would serve us well if we would focus on the Lord in our time of trouble, because He holds the answer to our many needs. He has promised to help those that need help.

- **"For he shall deliver the needy when he crieth; the poor also, and him that hath no helper." (Ps 72:12 KJV)**

The above offer is what I call an open-ended promise. It covers, needy, poor and the one that had no helper. That takes in everyone and the key is to cry out for help. Here again the tongue is used to produce good. We could use the tongue to call upon the Lord for help. He knows that we need help, but He expects us to cry out when we want it. The list is long for the services that our Lord renders and we can activate His services by the use of our voices.

We do not know all of the things David did to encourage himself but we can be sure that he used his voice. I arrived at this conclusion by the things that I can read in the Bible.

- **"I will bless the LORD at all times: his praise shall continually be in my mouth." (Ps 34:1 KJV)**

David knew from experience that praising the Lord was the best medicine that one could take and the more it is taken the less influence the enemy would have to defeat a God praiser.

It is always a blessing for ones ears to hear his or her mouth say what God's word is saying. To practice saying what the word says is a sure way of encouraging oneself.

- "Let my mouth be filled with thy praise and with thy honour all the day." (Ps 71:8 KJV)
- "And my tongue shall speak of thy righteousness and of thy praise all the day long." (Ps 35:28 KJV)
- "Deliver me from bloodguiltiness, O God, thou God of my salvation: and my tongue shall sing aloud of thy righteousness.
- 15 O Lord, open thou my lips; and my mouth shall shew forth thy praise." (Ps 51:14-15 KJV)
- "I will extol thee, my God, O king; and I will bless thy name for ever and ever.
- 2 Every day will I bless thee; and I will praise thy name for ever and ever." (Ps 145:1-2 KJV)
- "While I live will I praise the LORD: I will sing praises unto my God while I have any being."(Ps 146:2 KJV)

The scripture said that David was greatly distressed or troubled. When we read in the Bible, we can see what one should do when he or she is distressed. That is a good time to call upon the Lord for help.

> "In my distress I cried unto the LORD, and he heard me." (Ps 120:1 KJV)
>
> "In my distress I called upon the LORD, and cried unto my God: he heard my voice out of his temple, and my cry came before him, even into his ears." (Ps 18:6 KJV)
>
> "I called upon the LORD in distress: the LORD answered me, and set me in a large place." (Ps 118:5 KJV)

The preceding scriptures are good examples of right words turning things around. We should not hesitate when there is a need, and we should call upon the Lord with our whole heart until we get an answer.

It is high time that every believer should discover that praising the Lord has great benefits. We know that the Lord is glorified, but we seem to overlook the fact that we are edified through offering unto the Lord thanksgiving and praise.

I strongly believe that the enemy fears our prayers and our praise because he knows that both deeds are known to get God involved. He fears anything that ushers in the presence of the Lord. That is why he tries to bombard our minds with evil thoughts of doubt, fear, and discouragement. He wants to prevent us from receiving all that God has for us.

Satan has been an eyewitness of much deliverance of souls he thought he had for sure, but they commenced to call upon the Lord and were delivered from his clutches.

It was not just a coincidence that Paul and Silas prayed and sang praises at midnight. They were familiar with the scriptures. They knew how to usher in the presence of the Lord and where the Spirit of the Lord is there is sure to be deliverance.

Our God is on duty twenty four-seven, because He never slumbers or sleeps. His ears are open to the cry of the righteous, He is sure to hear when they cry.

- **"And at midnight Paul and Silas prayed, and sang praises unto God: and the prisoners heard them." (Acts 16:25 KJV)**
- **"Yet the LORD will command his lovingkindness in the daytime, and in the night**

his song shall be with me, and my prayer unto the God of my life." (Ps 42:8 KJV)
- "I call to remembrance my song in the night: I commune with mine own heart: and my spirit made diligent search." (Ps 77:6 KJV)
- "I have remembered thy name, O LORD, in the night, and have kept thy law." (Ps 119:55 KJV)
- "At midnight I will rise to give thanks unto thee because of thy righteous judgments." (Ps Ps 119:62 KJV)
- "And call upon me in the day of trouble: I will deliver thee, and thou shalt glorify me." (Ps 50:15 KJV)
- "He shall call upon me, and I will answer him: I will be with him in trouble; I will deliver him, and honour him." (Ps 91:15 KJV)

When ones mouth is filled with right words and especially when it is filled with God's word, all the demons between here and hell won't be able to keep the Lord from making His presence known.

The Word of God extends an invitation to call Him when we are in trouble. This proposition comes with a guarantee that He will be with us in trouble and that He will deliver, what more could one ask?

Since the enemy has seen this system work against him so often, he tries to overload us with troubles, hardship, difficulties, and burdens and pains hoping that we would be too heavy to cry for help but when we feed on God's word, we are sure to make application of His divine truth by calling out for help. When we approach the Lord with right words we can be sure that we would get His undivided attention because He is known to honor His word.

GETTING BACK TO GOD WITH RIGHT WORDS

- "O Israel, return unto the LORD thy God; for thou hast fallen by thine iniquity.
- 2 Take with you words, and turn to the LORD: say unto him, Take away all iniquity, and receive us graciously: so will we render the calves of our lips." (Hos 14:1-2 KJV)

Since we know that the Lord is no respecter of person, we know that He wouldn't tell one to do something that would help him or her and leave others outside of that same protection. He tells Israel that had been crushed by their sins, to return with right words. Since right words would reinstate Israel, I believe the same method would help us.

I am sure that we know that the Lord is above the possibility of being hoodwinked or bamboozled, so that means our words must be genuine and sincere. When we are troubled by drifting from the favor of the Lord and our hearts truly desire to be restored to full fellowship, the Lord would have respect of our words. God has always been known to grant repentance and then honor it when it is put into practice.

He tells Israel to make a request that their sins would be taken away, because sin is the main thing that stands between God and man. If man is willing to give up the sin practice, he need to approach the Lord with right words. He needs to ask the Lord to remove his sins and replace them with His presence.

We must credit the Lord for giving man the right words that are known to get His attention. This is another demonstration of His divine love for the human race. The words that a repentant person should approach the Lord with are words that request the removal of sins. It is after sins have been dealt with that one is qualified to offer unto the Lord the fruit of his lips. That is the kind of sacrifice that is acceptable to the Lord. The cross has made it possible for us to always have something to thank the Lord for.

Again let me say, it is more to returning to the Lord than just empty words. The words must be sincere and backed by action. There must be a putting away of the things that drew us away in the first place. When we return to the Lord, we must not bring with us the things that took us away in the past.

The words spoken by Samuel to Israel in his day are befitting for all returnees. The thing that would differ would all depend on the person or persons because not all forsake the Lord for the same things. Whatever drew one away, he or she must forsake it and then return.

A desire to return to the Lord is the true sign that one has repented. If one should do less that would indicate that a person was playing games. The Lord has no room for playing.

"And Samuel spake unto all the house of Israel, saying, If ye do return unto the LORD with all your hearts, then put away the strange gods and Ashtaroth from among you, and prepare your hearts unto the LORD, and serve him only: and he will deliver you out

> of the hand of the Philistines. Then the children of Israel did put away Baalim and Ashtaroth, and served the LORD only." (1 Sam 7:3-4 KJV)

Whenever we turn from the Lord, He expects His children to devote their lives to Him and Him alone. To do other wise would be less than what He has in mind for true discipleship.

When we truly repent, we draw the Lord's full support and protection. It is true repentance that brings things back to God's original order, and it has always been His delight to have His people near Him. Sin has always been a divider and always will be one, because the Lord will never agree with sinning and sinning will never fully satisfy man's thirst for fulfillment.

> "So the posts went with the letters from the king and his princes throughout all Israel and Judah, and according to the commandment of the king, saying, Ye children of Israel, turn again unto the LORD God of Abraham, Isaac, and Israel, and he will return to the remnant of you, that

> **are escaped out of the hand of the kings of Assyria.**
>
> **7 And be not ye like your fathers, and like your brethren, which trespassed against the LORD God of their fathers, who therefore gave them up to desolation, as ye see.**
>
> **8 Now be ye not stiffnecked, as your fathers were, but yield yourselves unto the LORD, and enter into his sanctuary, which he hath sanctified for ever: and serve the LORD your God, that the fierceness of his wrath may turn away from you.**
>
> **9 For if ye turn again unto the LORD, your brethren and your children shall find compassion before them that lead them captive, so that they shall come again into this land: for the LORD your God is gracious and merciful, and will not turn away his face from you, if ye return unto him." (2 Chron 30:6-9 KJV)**

When we fall into sin, the enemy would have us to smother in shame, pride, self-pity and disgrace. However, the Lord leaves the door open for man's return because He is longsuffering and full of mercy.

He is not willing that any should perish. That is why He grants repentance.

When a man repents of his errors, the door for a happy reunion swings open. God gets what He wants and man receives what he needs and that is, a God on his side. This makes for a happy reunion. Man is at home and the Father is happy for his return.

- **"Seek ye the LORD while he may be found, call ye upon him while he is near:**
- **7 Let the wicked forsake his way, and the unrighteous man his thoughts: and let him return unto the LORD, and he will have mercy upon him; and to our God, for he will abundantly pardon." (Isa 55:6-7 KJV)**

When sin bothers us enough to cry out to the Lord, it must also trouble us enough to cause us to turn away from the thing or things that brought about our departure in the first place. When we are sincere about giving up the wrong for the right, it is then and only then that we are in a position to draw upon His grace and mercy to receive pardon.

When we approach the Lord with His word, we are sure to gain an audience with Him because He is known to respect His word. That is why a person acting on the Word of God can do so with confidence. When God's word is proclaimed and the hearer lines up his or her life with the word, God is sure to get involved and what He has promised, He is sure to bring it to pass.

- **"Go and proclaim these words toward the north, and say, Return, thou backsliding Israel, saith the LORD; and I will not cause mine anger to fall upon you: for I am merciful, saith the LORD, and I will not keep anger for ever. 13 Only acknowledge thine iniquity, that thou hast transgressed against the LORD thy God, and hast scattered thy ways to the strangers under every green tree, and ye have not obeyed my voice, saith the LORD.**
- **14 Turn, O backsliding children, saith the LORD; for I am married unto you: and I will take you one of a city, and two of a family, and I will bring you to Zion:" (Jer 3:12-14 KJV)**

When we fall from grace but are willing to admit our blunder, if we would then turn to the Lord with right words, His ears are open to our cry. We must acknowledge our sins to the Lord, that is, if we expect Him to get involved with our restoration. When we admit that we have failed, that allows the Lord to put our sins behind Him and restore us back to our position of favor.

When we cry out to the Lord in our time of trouble, we are doing exactly what He expects us to do. In fact, He told us to call Him in our time of trouble. The time of trouble is a good time to make proper use of our tongue, by crying to the one that is listening for our cry.

- **"For he shall deliver the needy when he crieth; the poor also, and him that hath no helper." (Ps 72:12 KJV)**

What more encouragement should we need? We are told that we should call Him in our day of trouble. He knows that trouble is sure to come. Therefore, He tells us what to do
when it occurs. We should make our call count by calling Him. The call in the time of trouble could

be looked upon as God's 911. I promise you that His capability to quickly respond is much better than the fire department, police or hospital. He doesn't have to travel as far as any of the above.

- **"God is our refuge and strength, a very present help in trouble.**
- **2 Therefore will not we fear, though the earth be removed, and though the mountains be carried into the midst of the s**

Our God is a present helper. In other words, He doesn't have to come from any place because there is no place that He is not. Since He is so near, all He has to do is make His presence known. When He manifests Himself, Everything else has to fall in line with His demands.

It is a good thing to consult the Word of God on a subject matter, because mankind has been given a picture of God that doesn't fit the scriptures. We can be sure that our Lord is under no obligation to back what He hasn't spoken, or that which is out of line with what He has said.

- **"If thou wilt return, O Israel, saith the LORD, return unto me: and if thou wilt put away thine abominations out of my sight, then shalt thou not remove." (Jer 4:1 KJV)**

  "Therefore also now, saith the LORD, turn ye even to me with all your heart, and with fasting, and with weeping, and with mourning:
- **13 And rend your heart, and not your garments, and turn unto the LORD your God: for he is gracious and merciful, slow to anger, and of great kindness, and repenteth him of the evil." (Joel 2:12-13 KJV)**

I purposely stress action because words produce action. A person usually speaks before he or she acts. The actions of a person are often the fruit of what that person has been saying. We have in Hosea an appeal for the returnees to bring right words. In other places, they are basically told to turn and to let go of their evil doings. It is the kind of action that represents one desiring to be restored to divine fellowship.

TONGUE CONTROL, A SIGN OF STRENGTH

According to the Bible, the tongue is the most difficult member of the family to manage. When one can manage his or her words, it is truly a sign of great strength. The truth of the matter, the Lord is the only one that can give us what we need to bring the tongue under control. It takes more than human effort to maintain genuine control over the mouth.

The Word of God has much to say about tongue management. It offers sound advice about when to speak and when to hold one's peace. We just need to make application of this wonderful information.

According to the Word of God, knowing when to keep your words to yourself could be a sign of great strength and wisdom. Because to talk out of turn could lead to war, bitterness, hatred, animosity or the separation of the best of friends or loved ones.

- **"In the multitude of words there wanteth not sin: but he that refraineth his lips is wise." (Prov 10:19 KJV)**
- **"He that hath knowledge spareth his words: and a man of understanding is of an excellent spirit.**
- **28 Even a fool, when he holdeth his peace, is counted wise: and he that shutteth his lips is esteemed a man of understanding." (Prov 17:27-28 KJV)**

I have often said that person who talks excessively should either be highly educated, or they may run the risk of being a mighty big liar or both. The use of multitudes of words that are not carefully monitored can cause much harm to many lives. That is why tongue management is so essential, we want our words to minister grace to the hearers.

The wisdom of the word is profound. The Lord says that one knowing when to hold his peace would be considered wise. It sure would be wonderful if more people would believe God's word when it comes to mouth control, because many of us need to give our tongues some rest. At the same time we would give our neighbor's ears some needed rest.

It is too bad that we live in a society that feeds on useless and empty words. A person involved in entertainment such singing, rapping, or joking, these personalities are paid big bucks for speaking useless words. They are so influential that the spirit of entertainment has come into the church of the living God. We have men and women that make light of the Word of God. When the spirit of entertainment takes over, these speakers then offer the followers a substitute gospel one that won't offend, affect or change one's lifestyle.

The kind of preaching we hear as a whole could be called misuse of the mouth, because the mouth is supposed to be used for the glory of God, but the majority are using the tongue to tickle the ears of people.

The Apostle Paul felt it necessary to ask the saints to pray for his mouth. He wanted to say the right thing at the right time. His concern was to help someone. He didn't just want to utter words just to hear himself talk.

- **"Praying always with all prayer and supplication in the Spirit, and watching thereunto with all perseverance and supplication for all saints;**
- **19 And for me, that utterance may be given unto me, that I may open my mouth boldly, to make known the mystery of the gospel," (Eph 6:18-19 KJV)**

I don't know of anything that needs special prayer more than the preacher's mouth. The words that come out of his or her mouth need to have divine approval because the souls of men are depending on what comes out of the preacher's mouth. Too much is at stake for the preacher to just offer his or her opinion. We need the living Word of God. The word is the only thing that could bring about the change that we so desperately need.

The Lord expects His spokesperson to speak His word. He did not call us to give people our own misguided ideologies. Human thinking falls short when it comes to life changing ability. We need genuine change and the Word of God is the only source that can make that possible.

- **"The prophet that hath a dream, let him tell a dream; and he that hath my word, let him speak my word faithfully. What is the chaff to the wheat? saith the LORD.**
- **29 Is not my word like as a fire? saith the LORD; and like a hammer that breaketh the rock in pieces?" (Jer 23:28-29 KJV)**

The preaching and teaching of the true unadulterated Word of God is greatly missing in our midst today. We have too many that are influenced by popular opinion. They seem more concerned about pleasing the crowd than they are about pleasing the Creator of the universe.

When the word is not preached the genuine fire will be absent. That leaves us waning or seeing by false flames. It is little wonder that we are seeing great measures of worldly activities being carried out in the house of God.

Many of the sinful practices that are destroying the world have made it way to the church. I mean such sins as divorcing without Bible grounds, sexual misconduct, drunkenness, verbal and physical abuse, just to name a few. We are seeing today things practiced by church people that were once shameful in the alley. They are now center stage in the church.

I do not believe that the scriptures teach that we should be silent when it comes to delivering God's word. I read that we should cry aloud and spare not our voices should make a blast like a trumpet.

There are times when we should practice strict tongue control. It could be the difference between life and death.

- **"He that keepeth his mouth keepeth his life: but he that openeth wide his lips shall have destruction." (Prov 13:3 KJV)**
- **"He who guards his lips guards his life,**
- **but he who speaks rashly will come to ruin. "(From NIV)**

It has been said that "loose lips will wreck ships." Not only will a loose tongue wreck ship, it will turn one's life up side down or create more trouble in five minutes than one could overcome in a lifetime.

When we are surrounded by sinners or unbelievers or weak saints, we should be extremely careful what we say because our words have meaning. We should want to influence the weak and not be like them. It would serve us well to consider the fact that some of the same things that are in the weak are in us also. We don't want our mouth to ignite our weakness at a time we should be extending help.

- **"I said, "I will watch my ways**
- **and keep my tongue from sin;**
- **I will put a muzzle on my mouth**
- **as long as the wicked are in my presence." (Ps 39:1from NIV)**

When we complain, murmur, criticize others, gossip or overly engage ourselves in other people business, we can damage a person that is already weak or lost. We must guard our tongues in the presence of the unsaved and the spiritually unstable.

It is commonly believed that a person's brilliance is seen through the multitude of words when he or she speaks, but there is a time when a person's silence could speak for him. Knowing when to hold your peace is as important as knowing when to speak. I am sure that the more one knows, the more difficult it would be to remain silent.

- **"In the multitude of words there wanteth not sin: but he that refraineth his lips is wise." (Prov 10:19 KJV)**

I am a firm believer that the more we talk outside of God's word, the greater our risk of crossing the line and end up either lying or talking too much about little or nothing.

James calls the tongue a fire it can set the world aflame with few words. That is why knowing when to utter words is valuable to one's life and future.

There are people that don't like unnecessary trouble to the degree that they are willing to control their tongue. These people that live by such high standards are truly blessed and are known for diverting much trouble.

According to the Apostle James, a person's tongue gives an indication of the realness of his or her spirituality. I remember as a child, I would see the older people pick up a chicken that appeared to be sick. They would look in his mouth, especially the chicken's tongue, and they would treat his tongue. In a few days that chicken would be back to normal.

Just the thought they knew to look in the chicken's mouth, helps me to better understand James. He is telling me if I want to know the spiritual condition of a person, I should wait until he or she open his or her mouth.

- **"If any man among you seem to be religious, and bridleth not his tongue, but deceiveth his own heart, this man's religion is vain." (James 1:26 KJV)**

It is of utmost importance that believers keep strict control over the tongue, because the last thing we should want to happen is our spirituality be found useless and void.

The Bible has already informed us that believing that a thing is right to an individual doesn't mean that it is right with God, because God and man don't see things alike but God's view is always right.

- **"There is a way which seemeth right unto a man, but the end thereof are the ways of death." (Prov 14:12 KJV)**
- **"There is a way that seemeth right unto a man, but the end thereof are the ways of death." (Prov 16:25 KJV)**

The Word of God warns us not to be like a horse or mule that has to have a bit in its mouth to control it. We shouldn't need such cruel tactics to control our tongue or behavior. Our love for peace and goodwill should be all that we would need to keep us behaving like God-fearing people.

We are commanded to control our tongues. The Lord gives us this command knowing that the tongue is a deadly member of the family. It has a great potential for good but is also carrying the potential to create evil. That is why we must keep the tongue under control.

It has been said by some that words don't matter; however, the Lord says differently. He says that a person is responsible for every word he or she speaks.

- **"A good man out of the good treasure of the heart bringeth forth good things: and an evil man out of the evil treasure bringeth forth evil things.**
- **36 But I say unto you, That every idle word that men shall speak, they shall give account thereof in the day of judgment.**

- **37 For by thy words thou shalt be justified, and by thy words thou shalt be condemned." (Matt 12:35-37 KJV)**

There is absolutely nothing about us that reveals our contents like the tongue. It is known to reveal what's in the heart. It is true that we don't know what's in a person's heart, but if we wait long enough we would soon find out because the mouth would reveal what was in the heart by speaking.

The words that we speak are observed by the Master. We are sure to see the words that we have uttered will make our future either bright or gloomy.

I have often said, "He that thinks before speaking speaks well, but he that speaks before thinking is subject to say anything." The Bible says that we should be swift or quick to hear but slow to speak. This warning is given in light of the fact that the more we talk, the greater the risk of saying more than necessary.

The control of one's tongue is a strong indicator of his or her ability to manage his or her body. It is a sign of maturity.

- **"For in many things we offend all. If any man offend not in word, the same is a perfect man, and able also to bridle the whole body." (James 3:2 KJV)**

When we use our tongue for the right purpose, we are sure to bless someone else and at the same time glorify the Lord of glory.

Right words are like medicine, when they are spoken. They penetrate the depths of one's emotions and wake up the best in that person's spirit.

There comes a time when all people need to hear are the right words spoken in their ears. When those words are heard, they minister to our deepest needs and emotions. The places to look for right words are in the Word of God. The Lord gives us His word to pass on to others.

- **"My doctrine shall drop as the rain, my speech shall distil as the dew, as the small rain upon the tender herb, and as the showers upon the grass:" (Deut 32:2 KJV)**

- "A man hath joy by the answer of his mouth: and a word spoken in due season, how good is it!" (Prov 15:23 KJV)
- "Pleasant words are as an honeycomb, sweet to the soul, and health to the bones." (Prov 16:24 KJV)

  "Ointment and perfume rejoice the heart: so doth the sweetness of a man's friend by hearty counsel." (Prov 27:9 KJV)

The more a person loads his or her mouth with God's word, the more success he or she will have when it comes to speaking right words. Every tongue needs to speak right words, because the words that we speak can come back much sooner than we think. That is why it would be wise to put the right amount of honey in our words. Our own words may be our next meal.

SOME WORDS ANNOY GOD, BUT SOME ARE PLEASING TO HIM

As a rule we don't think or act as if the Lord has feelings. We just say and do as it pleases us we express the feelings that the Lord could take it or leave it. I would like to serve notice that the Lord has feelings there are things that annoys Him just as there are things that trouble us.

When the Lord tells us something and we act as if what He says doesn't matter, He is annoyed by that kind of attitude. The reason the Lord doesn't immediately wipe us out is because He is longsuffering and full of kindness. However, if we should continually take His goodness for granted, we will provoke Him to act in a manner that would put us in our place.

The best place to find examples of words that annoyed the Lord is in the Bible, because it has numerous examples to draw from.

The journey of the children of Israel Egypt to the promise land gives us several accounts where the Lord was annoyed with their attitudes and words. They spoke as if they were talking to Moses, but their words were basically to God. Moses just happened to be the one that they could see; therefore, they spoke to him what they wanted God to know.

The Psalmist gives us inside knowledge of what was really going on in the camp. He tells us who the target of the people's insults was.

- **19 "Yea, they spake against God; they said, Can God furnish a table in the wilderness?**
- **20 Behold, he smote the rock, that the waters gushed out, and the streams overflowed; can he give bread also? can he provide flesh for his people?**
- **21 Therefore the LORD heard this, and was wroth: so a fire was kindled against Jacob, and anger also came up against Israel;" (Ps 78:19-21 KJV)**

The Psalmist didn't say that they spoke against Moses. He said that they spoke against God. They questioned the Lord's ability to fulfill His word. It was the Lord that promised to provide for them and Moses was sent to lead them. Moses was there as God's contact person to help the people find their way. He was not sent to be their God, but to be God's representative to the people.

It would serve all leadership well if we would realize that we are God's representative to the people and not a God to the people. There are things we can do, but many things we cannot do. It is our responsibility to stay close enough to the Lord to know where our place begins and ends. If we attempt to take the Lord's place, the people will no longer have a leader, they would have a poor substitute of a god.

When the people complained the Bible says: **"Therefore the LORD heard this, and was wroth."** The thing about angering the Lord, He has so many ways to bring us down to size that it is impossible to fight with Him.

Israel was much like us today very short on memory. No matter how the Lord blesses us, we tend to forget His blessings. When trouble arises in our lives, we forget what He did the last time and focus on the thing that's at hand.

When we murmur and complain we are acting like Israel of old. Their journey from Egypt to the promised land was marked with complaints, doubts and fears. It was all because they didn't really believe the Lord.

- **"How oft did they provoke him in the wilderness, and grieve him in the desert!**
- **41 Yea, they turned back and tempted God, and limited the Holy One of Israel.**
- **42 They remembered not his hand, nor the day when he delivered them from the enemy.**
- **43 How he had wrought his signs in Egypt, and his wonders in the field of Zoan:" (Ps 78:40-43 KJV)**

God at one point had to get Moses' thinking back on track. I could suppose that his surroundings got to him and caused him to question God's ability to make good His word. The word tells us that evil communication corrupts good manners. The Lord didn't hesitate to let Moses know that He was the same God that Moses had seen work in Egypt and nothing had happened to His ability.

- **"But Moses said, "There are 600,000 men alone [besides all the women and children], and yet you promise them meat for a whole month! 22 If we butcher all our flocks and herds it won't be enough! We would have to catch every fish in the ocean to fulfill your promise!"**
- **23 Then the Lord said to Moses, "When did I become weak? Now you shall see whether my word comes true or not!" (Num 11:21-23 TLB)**

The next time you are tempted to feel that God can no longer fulfill His promises remember His reply to Moses. He has not become weak, He is yet God and faith in Him would open the way for getting the job done.

When God sends His word, He expects the hearers of the word to believe Him because He never speaks what He cannot perform. Getting His word on a things is a guarantee that no one or nothing can stop from coming to pass.

It doesn't matter what the circumstances are, when the Lord speaks, He has what it takes to fulfill His word.

- **"Then Elisha said, Hear ye the word of the LORD; Thus saith the LORD, To morrow about this time shall a measure of fine flour be sold for a shekel, and two measures of barley for a shekel, in the gate of Samaria." (2 Kings 7:1 KJV)**

God sent His much-needed word during a severe famine. He sent them words of hope words that should have raised the people to a level of expectancy. God didn't consult with the famine. He just said what would be in about a twenty-four hour period. I am sure that the man of God had no visible evidence to support such claims, but he had faith in the God that sent him to say what he said and that was enough for him.

God's word did not find everyone ready to receive it. There will always be some doubters in every gathering. The sad thing is the doubters seem to have the loudest voice and the longest conversation, and they feel that they must be heard.

- **"Then a lord on whose hand the king leaned answered the man of God, and said, Behold, if the LORD would make windows in heaven, might this thing be? And he said, Behold, thou shalt see it with thine eyes, but shalt not eat thereof." (2 Kings 7:2 KJV)**

The Lord leaves a variety of examples in His word to teach us. If we would only learn from the mistakes of others, we would avoid making the same blunders.

The lord in the preceding text sounded much like the other negative talkers he called into question God's ability to fulfill His word. That is a sure way of bringing His swift judgment down on you.

The man of God told him that his eyes would see it but his mouth wouldn't taste it. This man talked himself into an untimely death. He proved that death was in his tongue. It would have been good had he just keep his mouth shut since he didn't seem to have the right words to say.

This man is a typical example of one being in the right place at the right time, but allows his mouth bring death rather than life upon him. He was not the only one that heard the message. He was the only one that voiced his doubt about its fulfillment, the others maintained silence. This fulfilled the scripture that says: **"Even a fool, when he holdeth his peace, is counted wise: and he that shutteth his lips is esteemed a man of understanding." (Prov 17:28 KJV)**

There is yet more to this intriguing story. There were four men that would be considered outcasts who were near the entering of the gate. They had a disease that kept them from being included in their society.

These four leprous men were in the right place at the right time, to both save their lives and the lives of others. They are a good example that the Lord can use whomever He chooses, and they don't have to be in the main stream for Him to bless them. Sometimes, the very ones that are overlooked by the majority are the very ones that could cause a change.

- **"And there were four leprous men at the entering in of the gate: and they said one to another, Why sit we here until we die?**
- **4 If we say, We will enter into the city, then the famine is in the city, and we shall die**

there: and if we sit still here, we die also. Now therefore come, and let us fall unto the host of the Syrians: if they save us alive, we shall live; and if they kill us, we shall but die.

- 5 And they rose up in the twilight, to go unto the camp of the Syrians: and when they were come to the uttermost part of the camp of Syria, behold, there was no man there.
- 6 For the Lord had made the host of the Syrians to hear a noise of chariots, and a noise of horses, even the noise of a great host: and they said one to another, Lo, the king of Israel hath hired against us the kings of the Hittites, and the kings of the Egyptians, to come upon us.
- 7 Wherefore they arose and fled in the twilight, and left their tents, and their horses, and their asses, even the camp as it was, and fled for their life.
- 8 And when these lepers came to the uttermost part of the camp, they went into one tent, and did eat and drink, and carried thence silver, and gold, and raiment,

and went and hid it; and came again, and entered into another tent, and carried thence also, and went and hid it.
- 9 Then they said one to another, We do not well: this day is a day of good tidings, and we hold our peace: if we tarry till the morning light, some mischief will come upon us: now therefore come, that we may go and tell the king's household.
- 10 So they came and called unto the porter of the city: and they told them, saying, We came to the camp of the Syrians, and, behold, there was no man there, neither voice of man, but horses tied, and asses tied, and the tents as they were.
- 11 And he called the porters; and they told it to the king's house within." (2 Kings 7:3-11 KJV)

We know that being in the right place at the right time doesn't necessary mean that a person would do the right thing. but in this case, they reasoned among themselves that it was best to share what they had found.

Their decision to go into the camp of the enemy was propelled by right words. They reasoned that death is but death. If they remained there, it would come and if the Syrians killed them so what. The question they posed to each other is a searching one: "Why sit we here until we die?" They knew death would come but it didn't have to find them sitting idlely by, it could find them trying to live.

They considered their choices. If they remained there, they would die. If they went into the city where the famine had taken its toll, they would die there. They chose the other option, they decided to go into the camp of the Syrians and take their chances. This proved to be the wise move.

- **"If we say, We will enter into the city, then the famine is in the city, and we shall die there: and if we sit still here, we die also. Now therefore come, and let us fall unto the host of the Syrians: if they save us alive, we shall live; and if they kill us, we shall but die." (2 Kings 7:4 KJV)**

The words of these dying men were laced with hope. They were determined not to just sit there and die, and they thought it best to put forth some effort to live. We should draw a line from these men and pursue life instead of death. We should fill our mouth with words that promote life and discard the word that supports death.

- **'I shall not die, but live, and declare the works of the LORD.' (Ps 118:17 KJV)**

I am convinced that everyday the Lord allows us to be awake, that we should spend our time seeking what He wants from us that day. Even if we are sick, we should not cater to our feelings. We should talk life.

When we resume the story of the promise of God in the time of famine, we see that the words of the lepers were not taken at face value. The king sent investigators to check out their story.

I suppose the king felt that the story sounded too good to be true. He felt that it could have been a trap set by the Syrians to lure them outside the city so that they could finish them off.

They didn't know that the Lord was at work to make good His word that was spoken by His servant Elisha. When God gives us a promise, He knows how it is going to come to pass. All we need is to believe Him and act like He meant what He said.

Elijah told that doubting critic that his eyes would see but his tongue wouldn't taste it. As the fulfillment drew nearer we find the king checking things out to see if something good was coming their way.

- **"And they went after them unto Jordan: and, lo, all the way was full of garments and vessels, which the Syrians had cast away in their haste. And the messengers returned, and told the king." (2 Kings 7:15 KJV)**

The investigating committee returned with good news. They found things even as the lepers had said. The good news bought new life into the city. People that were preparing to die started thinking of living. The thing that seemed impossible twenty-four hours earlier was now looking very hopeful.

"And the people went out, and spoiled the tents of the Syrians. So a measure of fine flour was sold for a shekel, and two measures of barley for a shekel,

according to the word of the LORD." (2 Kings 7:16 KJV)

The Lord made good His word that was spoken by Elisha the prophet. The famine was unable to prevent the blessings of the Lord from reaching His people.

The Lord didn't just carry out a portion of His Word. He backed all that the man of God spoke, even the portion that pointed out that the doubter would see it, but wouldn't taste it.

The annoying words spoken by the kings' servant worked more against him than they did anyone else. The prophet told him just how close he would get, just close enough to see what happened, but not close enough to taste the blessing.

- **"And the king appointed the lord on whose hand he leaned to have the charge of the gate: and the people trode upon him in the gate, and he died, as the man of God had said, who spake when the king came down to him.**
- **18 And it came to pass as the man of God had spoken to the king, saying, Two mea-**

> sures of barley for a shekel, and a measure of fine flour for a shekel, shall be to morrow about this time in the gate of Samaria:
> - **19 And that lord answered the man of God, and said, Now, behold, if the LORD should make windows in heaven, might such a thing be? And he said, Behold, thou shalt see it with thine eyes, but shalt not eat thereof.**
> - **20 And so it fell out unto him: for the people trode upon him in the gate, and he died." (2 Kings 7:17-20 KJV)**

We need to learn from this annoying, doubting man that when the Lord speaks, even if we don't believe Him, we would be better off to keep our mouth shut and not provoke or annoy the Lord with our loose lips.

When we are speaking words of faith, we do not have to change our language because of prevailing conditions. At the time Elisha spoke God's word, the land was in a deep famine. We must decide in our hearts that God's word is true and right and nothing can change it or prevent its fulfillment. If the Devil could change God's word, you could be sure that he would, but there is nothing he can do to destroy God's word. Even he has to respect the Word of God.

The Shunammite woman is another good example of one speaking God pleasing words in the face of great odds. Walking by faith eliminates the need to consult circumstances. The only one we need to check with is the Lord. The Shunammite woman didn't describe her situation. It appears that she didn't even tell her husband that the child was dead. She just started preparing to go to the man of God, one that she felt could get an answer to pray.

I learned from this woman of faith how to focus when things are against you. Don't rehearse your problems. Just seek God's answer.

- **"And the woman conceived, and bare a son at that season that Elisha had said unto her, according to the time of life.**
- **And when the child was grown, it fell on a day, that he went out to his father to the reapers.**
- **And he said unto his father, My head, my head. And he said to a lad, Carry him to his mother.**

- **And when he had taken him, and brought him to his mother, he sat on her knees till noon, and then died." (2 Kings 4:17-20 KJV)**

This had to be a devastating blow to this woman. She had wanted a son for a long time. Now that she has one only to watch him succumb to death right before her very eyes. However, thank God, she did not accept his death as permanent. She felt that something could be done when she made contact with man of God that had predicted his beginning.

- **"And when he had taken him, and brought him to his mother, he sat on her knees till noon, and then died.**
- **21 And she went up, and laid him on the bed of the man of God, and shut the door upon him, and went out.**
- **22 And she called unto her husband, and said, Send me, I pray thee, one of the young men, and one of the asses, that I may run to the man of God, and come again.**
- **23 And he said, Wherefore wilt thou go to him to day? it is neither new moon, nor**

sabbath. And she said, It shall be well." (2 Kings 4:20-23 KJV)

Faith would not direct her to make funeral arrangements. A resurrection was the predominant thought in her heart and mind. To make that happen, she needed to run to the man of God. She needed a faith partner to assist in bringing about the miracle she needed. She didn't let her husband's question distract her from going: **"Wherefore wilt thou go to him to day? it is neither new moon, nor sabbath."** He was saying that her trip was out of time with the season or period. When one was supposed to go to the man of God, she was not thinking of times and seasons. She was thinking of a miracle being performed on her son. Notice her reply, **"And she said, It shall be well."** She spoke the words that ushered in the presence of God. She spoke what she believed and not what she saw. It appears that she didn't even tell her husband that the child was dead. It indicates that she believed that the child would be raised back to life. She didn't let tears, sobs, murmuring and complaining to cloud her mind and block her pursuit for help.

- "Then she saddled an ass, and said to her servant, Drive, and go forward; slack not thy riding for me, except I bid thee.
- 25 So she went and came unto the man of God to mount Carmel. And it came to pass, when the man of God saw her afar off, that he said to Gehazi his servant, Behold, yonder is that Shunammite:
- 26 Run now, I pray thee, to meet her, and say unto her, Is it well with thee? is it well with thy husband? is it well with the child? And she answered, It is well." (2 Kings 4:24-2 KJV)

We have heard the term "wouldn't take no for an answer." This woman could not conceive that the child that the Lord had miraculously given her could be gone forever. That is why she answered in faith by saying: "It is well." Faith sees what the natural eye cannot see or comprehend. Faith has divine help when it comes to assessing life's situations.

It is a Biblical fact that God honors faith. Wherever He finds it and in whomever He finds it. When one chooses to trust the Word of God, he or she can be sure that he or she would have the Lord's full support.

When I say that the Lord honors faith, wherever He finds it. I am saying that a person doesn't have to be from the camp of the chosen to have his or her faith supported by the Master.

In the days of Elijah, the land experienced a severe famine. The Lord looked outside the camp of the Israelites to find a provision for His servant. He sent him to a place where He knew faith abounded.

- **"Arise, get thee to Zarephath, which belongeth to Zidon, and dwell there: behold, I have commanded a widow woman there to sustain thee.**
- **10 So he arose and went to Zarephath. And when he came to the gate of the city, behold, the widow woman was there gathering of sticks: and he called to her, and said, Fetch me, I pray thee, a little water in a vessel, that I may drink.**
- **11 And as she was going to fetch it, he called to her, and said, Bring me, I pray thee, a morsel of bread in thine hand.**

- **12 And she said, As the LORD thy God liveth, I have not a cake, but an handful of meal in a barrel, and a little oil in a cruse: and, behold, I am gathering two sticks, that I may go in and dress it for me and my son, that we may eat it, and die.**
- **13 And Elijah said unto her, Fear not; go and do as thou hast said: but make me thereof a little cake first, and bring it unto me, and after make for thee and for thy son.**
- **14 For thus saith the LORD God of Israel, The barrel of meal shall not waste, neither shall the cruse of oil fail, until the day that the LORD sendeth rain upon the earth.**
- **15 And she went and did according to the saying of Elijah: and she, and he, and her house, did eat many days.**
- **16 And the barrel of meal wasted not, neither did the cruse of oil fail, according to the word of the LORD, which he spake by Elijah." (1 Kings 17:9-16 KJV)**

This is a very interesting story, because it highlights God's ability to work with a faith-filled person that happened to live outside the camp. You can be sure that she wasn't the only widow in community. She just happened to be the one that the Lord could use to sustain His servant. I love that word sustain: to give support or relief to, to supply with sustenance: nourish, to bear up under, to supply with nourishment, to put up with (something painful or difficult) (Merriam-Webster Thesaurus)

When the man of God arrived at the home of this widow woman, she had already been visited by God. You see, the Lord works on both ends. Just as He had prepared the faith of Elijah to such a place without fear or intimidation, He equally prepared the woman to handle her task of sustaining him. This is the word of the Lord: **"I have commanded a widow woman there to sustain thee."**

When the man of God arrived at the widow's house, he found her gathering some sticks to prepare her last meal before submitting to death. His first request was met with ease to her mind. She thought it a small thing to fetch the man of God some water, but he went to a step further. He added to his request. **"Fetch me, I pray thee, a little water in a vessel, that I may drink. And as she was going to fetch it, he called to her, and said, Bring me, I pray thee, a morsel of bread in thine hand."**

The Key To Your Future Is In Your Mouth

Even after one hears from the Lord, he or she yet has to make a conscience decision to obey. Knowing the Lord's will is not enough, we must be willing to trust and obey before it can take effect in us.

We must admit that the prophet presented a tall order to a woman, that had to think of her child as well as herself in the time of a famine. She was looking in a barrel that was all but depleted. It contained just enough to maybe suffice her and her child this once. Now she has to decide on sharing it with a total stranger and a man too. She could have easily used the brand of thinking most would have used. She could have decided to let him seek help somewhere else. After all, he's a man, and I am a woman with a child. However, God had His hand on the woman that was enough to awaken the faith that was in her heart to trust and obey the voice of the Lord.

The woman revealed that she had less than enough to make a whole cake. In fact, her hand could hold the little meal that she had and two sticks would be enough to cook what she had. The man of God told her to continue with her plan but fix him one first; that took real faith.

When faith is on trial, the Lord always sends His word to fortify our faith. The words that the prophet spoke to this widow woman were words that came from the mouth of God. When the Lord speaks, He takes personal responsibility in seeing that His word accomplishes what He pleases.

- **"For thus saith the LORD God of Israel, The barrel of meal shall not waste, neither shall the cruse of oil fail, until the day that the LORD sendeth rain upon the earth.**
- **And she went and did according to the saying of Elijah: and she, and he, and her house, did eat many days."**

The words that the man of God spoke in the widow's ears were much needed to support her in carrying out the plan of God, when she got the promise of God. She acted on the words spoken by the man of God that turned things around for her and the child. Remember, faith is not faith until it had been put to the test. When the woman responded to the prophet's request to give him a piece of her bread first, that was a real test. However, thank God that the woman who had been commanded to sustain the man of God passed the test with flying colors.

Her act of obedience got her ready for the next miracle. She lost her son temporally to death, but she believed that the man of God was in touch with the master; therefore, he could call upon the Lord and get an answer.

- **"And it came to pass after these things, that the son of the woman, the mistress of the house, fell sick; and his sickness was so sore, that there was no breath left in him.**
- **18 And she said unto Elijah, What have I to do with thee, O thou man of God? art thou come unto me to call my sin to remembrance, and to slay my son?**
- **19 And he said unto her, Give me thy son. And he took him out of her bosom, and carried him up into a loft, where he abode, and laid him upon his own bed.**
- **20 And he cried unto the LORD, and said, O LORD my God, hast thou also brought evil upon the widow with whom I sojourn, by slaying her son?**
- **21 And he stretched himself upon the child three times, and cried unto the LORD, and**

> said, O LORD my God, I pray thee, let this child's soul come into him again.
> - 22 And the LORD heard the voice of Elijah; and the soul of the child came into him again, and he revived.
> - 23 And Elijah took the child, and brought him down out of the chamber into the house, and delivered him unto his mother: and Elijah said, See, thy son liveth.
> - 24 And the woman said to Elijah, Now by this I know that thou art a man of God, and that the word of the LORD in thy mouth is truth." (1 Kings 17:17-24 KJV)

It is impossible to separate faith from obedience. Where you find one, you are sure to find the other. The woman in the beginning could be said to have acted in obedience, but after the death of her son and seeing him raised back to life, she could from that point forward act in faith.

The story ends with her knowing that Elijah was a man of God, one with the Word of God in his mouth. No greater compliment could be paid a servant of the Lord; no greater way can God's messengers distinguish himself or herself than to have His word in his or her mouth.

When we consider the story of Elijah and the widow woman, we must understand that it was not an automatic thing. It was faith in action where faith could be found. When the man of God spoke God's word to the widow woman, she could have done like many often do, she could have chosen to ignore God's word and do what she felt was best for her and the child. However, she heeded the word and followed the directions that were given by the prophet.

It appears that she didn't really know the prophet. She had never seen him perform, yet she obeyed the Word of God from his mouth. This woman had no visible evidence to support her action. All she had was the Word of God from the mouth of the prophet. Her actions demonstrated why the Lord chose her to work with His servant in carving out a story that has fed the faith of many.

I would feel remiss to omit the words that were spoken by the Lord Jesus on this subject. He pointed out that there were widows in Israel, but to none of them was His servant sent. That statement opens the door for many speculations. The question "why?" comes to mind, then the answer that is easiest to reach, the Lord knew the in-house attitude that existed among His chosen people.

The Lord demonstrated to us that He works with faith, wherever He finds it. It accomplishes His will for the lives of all that trust Him and obey His word.

I think it is sad when the Lord has to reach outside the church to find people to believe in His word, but if He has to, He will. He has demonstrated that fact many times over.

- **"But I tell you of a truth, many widows were in Israel in the days of Elias, when the heaven was shut up three years and six months, when great famine was throughout all the land;**
- **26 But unto none of them was Elias sent, save unto Sarepta, a city of Sidon, unto a woman that was a widow.**
- **27 And many lepers were in Israel in the time of Eliseus the prophet; and none of them was cleansed, saving Naaman the Syrian." (Luke 4:25-27 KJV)**

Jesus says it best by pointing out that miracles took place outside of camp of the Israelites, because faith was found other than among the chosen people.

While I am highlighting outsiders, we should consider the words of the woman that had the issue of blood. I am impressed with what she did, but more impressed with what she said before reaching the Master.

She faced a great challenge because of the period of time that she had suffered. She had to be weak from her condition, but she was determined to get her healing. She was so determined that she could no longer stay in the house. This woman sets a pattern for people that want to be healed or helped. They must be willing to spend all efforts to position themselves for the blessing that they seek.

She had concluded that the doctors couldn't do it and staying locked up in the house wouldn't bring healing. She decided that she would press her way to Jesus and get what she needed.

She made her move toward Jesus, after she had heard about Him. It was something that she heard that gave her courage to tackle the crowed and to ignore her feelings, while pursuing her faith.

One thing is for sure, acting in faith never makes sense. That is why the carnal mind looks upon the action of faith as crazy. When I passed out on the plane a few years ago, I was en route to Detroit from

Jackson, MS. By the time the plane leveled off, I passed out and when I came to myself, I was on my back in the center of the plane. They turned the plane around, took me back to Jackson, and rushed me to the nearest hospital. A young lady approached me with a clip board and asked me to sign on the bottom line. I asked her what was the signature for and she said to authorize the hospital to treat whatever they found wrong with me. I told her that I would sign only one thing and that would be something that would get me up out of there. The young lady quickly went out and passed my information to the doctor. He came in order to try his hand at getting me to remain there for observation, but my message was the same to him as it was to the nurse. I told them that I had to teach a class in Detroit the next day. There was no way that I could teach in Detroit lying in a hospital bed in Jackson, MS. I got dressed and headed to the nearest Wal-Mart to get me a shirt because the aisle of the plane was wet. I found me a buggy and bought a black striped shirt, that I call my victory shirt. I caught the next available flight to Detroit that afternoon and was there to teach my class the next day.

That wasn't the first time that I had walked away from medical advice. About eleven years ago, I had gone for a physical check-up and was told by the physician that I might have to have a pacemaker. When he said that, I asked them to pass me my jacket because I wasn't going to let the medical professionals kill me. I got my jacket and hit the door, I haven't been back to that doctor for anymore check-ups. I found one that checked me from head to toe, but found none of what the other doctor suggested.

I didn't wait to see before acting. I acted like I believed the moment the challenge presented itself. I know that I am going to die, but I sure don't intend to let anyone scare me to death with medical language. If the Lord wanted me dead all He has to do is withhold the next breath, and I would be gone and so would you.

The woman with the issue made up her mind to get to Jesus. This included getting through the crowd. Her determination was so strong that even the crowed couldn't deter her from pursuing after what she believed.

- **"When she had heard of Jesus, came in the press behind, and touched his garment.**
- **28 For she said, If I may touch but his clothes, I shall be whole.**

- **29 And straightway the fountain of her blood was dried up; and she felt in her body that she was healed of that plague.**
- **30 And Jesus, immediately knowing in himself that virtue had gone out of him, turned him about in the press, and said, Who touched my clothes?**
- **31 And his disciples said unto him, Thou seest the multitude thronging thee, and sayest thou, Who touched me?" (Mark 5:27-31 KJV)**

In this woman's condition, the best news for her to hear was Jesus was in her city, the same Jesus that was healing the sick, raising the dead, giving sight to the blind and causing the lame to walk again. That is the kind of news that builds faith and motivates one to go beyond self and touch the Savior.

It is a fact that if we touch Him, He is sure to touch us back and His touch brings change wherever it is needed. The woman that was healed reveals that one must have a made up mind in advance. He or she must believe that touching the Master would bring healing or a miracle. Better yet, it would bring wholeness: **"For she said, If I may touch but his clothes, I shall be whole."**

The faith of this woman drew out of Jesus' virtue, the moment she touched Him. He knew something wonderful had happened to someone in the midst. The woman didn't just brush against Him, she touched Him with her faith.

THE QUESTION OF THE HOUR
(Have you lifted as many as you have torn down?)

We have already observed that the tongue has a tremendous amount of power and influence. This why I raise the question, have you lifted as many as you have torn down? That is a question that all must answer. We may not have an exact number, one way or the other, but the question must be dealt with according to the Lord Jesus.

- **"But I say unto you, that every idle word that men shall speak, they shall give an account thereof in the day of judgment.**

- **For by thy words thou shalt be justified, and by thy words thou shalt be condemned." (Matt 12:36-37 KJV)**

I hope the fact that we cannot use our tongues any way we choose without consequences is clear in your minds. The Lord is listening to every word that comes out of our mouth, and He holds us responsible for the word we speak.

We may not know the answer to the question, "Have I lifted as many as I have torn down?" The Lord won't need a calculator to sum up the ways that my tongue was used. He already knows and He will be able to reveal to me that number in the end.

The Bible gives us ways in which the tongue could be used and the results that could be reached, but it is up to us how we use this wonderful gift.

It would be a good thing if I would use my tongue with glorifying the Lord in mind. That way I would never use it wrong or out of place. When we use the tongue according to its creative purpose, the Lord is honored and people are blessed.

- **"Out of the same mouth proceedeth blessing and cursing. My brethren, these things ought not so to be.**
- **Doth a fountain send forth at the same place sweet water and bitter?**
- **Can the fig tree, my brethren, bear olive berries? either a vine, figs? so can no fountain both yield salt water and fresh.**
- **Who is a wise man and endued with knowledge among you? let him shew out of a good conversation his works with meekness of wisdom." (James 3:10-13 KJV)**

James points out that the mouth has the potential to produce two opposite things. It is not as faithful as a fountain that never sends forth two kinds of water at the same time or a fig tree that is totally devoted to bearing figs only. The fountain doesn't offer two kinds of water at the same time, if you want salt water don't expect it from the fountain that is given to fresh water.

James tells us that a person's use of the tongue reveals his wisdom and knowledge. One that uses his tongue to build people up is a wise person and one that is in touch with the Master of good things.

The good conversation that James talks about goes far beyond words. It deals with lifestyle, conduct and character. However, one can commence to detect what's in a person by listening to him of her. The tongue is one of our strongest indicators, it is known to reveal to the eye what's in the heart?

We have observed earlier that the holding of one's peace could make one appear wise, a person of understanding.

- **"Even a fool, when he holdeth his peace, is counted wise: and he that shutteth his lips is esteemed a man of understanding." (Prov 17:28 KJV)**
- **That passage should help us when we are tempted to talk negative and critical language, we should be reminded that we belong to the Lord, we shouldn't have to listen to messages that tear people down.**
- **"But the tongue can no man tame; it is an unruly evil, full of deadly poison." (James 3:8 KJV)**

When the Word of God states the fact that no man can tame the tongue, I feel reasonably sure that He is not saying that it cannot be done; He is saying that no man could do it. There are many things that man cannot alone do, but through the help of the Lord that which would be impossible, becomes possible when we allow the Lord to help us.

A wise person knows that it is best to keep control of the tongue when he or she is surrounded by wickedness. The reason for maintaining mouth control is every one of us has some of the same things dwelling in us that the wicked has in them. If we fail to take control, it is a known fact that we are subject to fall victim of their influence.

- **"Be not deceived: evil communications corrupt good manners." (1 Cor 15:33 KJV)**

No matter how pure our intentions may be, if we don't guard our thoughts and tongue, we are subject to fall victim of evil behavior.

We can be sure that there are people that bring the best out of us, as well as there are those that bring out the worst. It is our responsibility keep watch over our responses to all around us.

- **"I said, I will take heed to my ways, that I sin not with my tongue: I will keep my mouth with a bridle, while the wicked is before me." (Ps 39:1 KJV)**

It pays to think before opening your mouth. When you are surrounded by people that tend to be loose in their speaking, because words are somewhat like cancer, it doesn't take them long to spread, and once they are out, it is impossible to undue the damage that wrong words could cause.

Notice the recommendation the word offers: **"I will keep my mouth with a bridle, while the wicked is before me."** If you know anything about horses, you know that the instrument listed in our text is used to control the behavior of a horse. This strong animal is too powerful to contain by putting something on his legs, tail or ears. You need to put something in his mouth. If you don't control his mouth, you don't direct him. When the wicked are before us, we need to put the teachings of the Bible in our mouth to control it. We need to be reminded that our soul is a risk.

- **"He that keepeth his mouth keepeth his life: but he that openeth wide his lips shall have destruction." (Prov 13:3 KJV)**
- **"In the multitude of words there wanteth not sin: but he that refraineth his lips is wise." (Prov 10:19 KJV)**
- **"Whoso keepeth his mouth and his tongue keepeth his soul from troubles." (Prov 21:23 KJV)**

It should be in the forefront of our minds and heart to use our tongue in a manner that God would be glorified and man would be edified. When we devote our tongues to the use of blessing God and refreshing man, we develop a pleasant atmosphere, one that the soul of men could cherish.

To make our words count, we must act on the teachings of the Bible. We cannot allow both types of messages to proceed out of our mouth; we are in the mental and spiritual construction business. Our job is to build up; our tongues should be ready at all times to give good advice, encouragement, inspiration, motivation, wisdom, knowledge and hope. Believers should never employ their mouth for destructive ends. We are in Christ's stead, and we need to use our tongues to bring life and not death.

- **"Let no corrupt communication proceed out of your mouth, but that which is good to the use of edifying, that it may minister grace unto the hearers." (Eph 4:29 KJV)**

It is plainly stated that we are not to use our mouth to carry garbage, filth, bitterness, hatred, criticism, gossip or any other soul-vexing words or deeds; we are to start at the ground level and build people up.

You know as well as I do that the Bible would not issue such a warning if the possibility didn't exist. The Lord wants us to avoid using our tongues for negative purposes. He wants us to use our tongues to create better conditions for others and to glorify His name.

We must not sweep under the rug the fact that the tongue carries a twofold potential. It can do much good as well as much evil, but by the help of the Lord, we want our tongues to engage in good.

- "Thy tongue deviseth mischiefs; like a sharp rasor, working deceitfully." (Ps 52:2 KJV)
- "O generation of vipers, how can ye, being evil, speak good things? for out of the abundance of the heart the mouth speaketh.
- 35 A good man out of the good treasure of the heart bringeth forth good things: and an evil man out of the evil treasure bringeth forth evil things." (Matt 12:34-35 KJV)

Just as evil men use their tongues to cause hurt and harm to others, we must use ours to bring refreshing and hope. It would be wise if every word we spoke was carefully monitored and laced with the right seasoning so that the recipients would find delight in what we say. That is the ministry we are in, and we should practice with great diligence.

- "Let your speech be alway with grace, seasoned with salt, that ye may know how ye ought to answer every man." (Col 4:6 KJV)

When we speak God favorite and compassionately flavored words, the recipients of such words are edified. In other words, our words must fall in line with God's word, proceeding out of a heart that is godly concerned in order to benefit the hearers.

- **"The mouth of the righteous speaketh wisdom, and his tongue talketh of judgment.**
- **31 The law of his God is in his heart; none of his steps shall slide." (Ps 37:30-31 KJV)**

We should never disappoint people when we stand to speak or when we hold a conversation with them. We should not give the words that would add to their already down condition. We should have a word that would serve as an elevator. Our words should be able to bring a person from the basement and take them to the penthouse.

When we minister to the needs of others with right words, we solidify our own status with the Lord. Note what the word says: **"The law of his God is in his heart; none of his steps shall slide."** Speaking God's word in a right manner anchors our position in

Him, and we need to be secure in a desired position, so that every wind won't blow us from side to side.

I pray to God that every minister of the gospel would get the revelation of the value of preaching and teaching the unadulterated Word of God. We need a glimpse of what it does for the hearers, as well as what it does for the speaker.

- **"I have preached righteousness in the great congregation: lo, I have not refrained my lips, O LORD, thou knowest.**
- **I have not hid thy righteousness within my heart; I have declared thy faithfulness and thy salvation: I have not concealed thy lovingkindness and thy truth from the great congregation." (Ps 40:9-10 KJV)**

One of the main reasons that we should speak God's word faithfully, the Lord takes full responsibility in seeing that His word accomplishes what He has spoken. When we give something to a person by the name of God's word, He is under no obligation to support what we say, but when we speak in agreement with His word, He will back it every time.

Another reason we need to speak God's word to people is His word is spirit and life. If we hope to make people better, we need to use that which is designed to reach the desired end.

- **"It is the spirit that quickeneth; the flesh profiteth nothing: the words that I speak unto you, they are spirit, and they are life." (John 6:63 KJV)**

When we speak to people after the flesh, we can only hope to achieve that which the flesh produces. But when we speak God's word, we would be using that which begets life. That is why we need to fill our mouth with God's word. When we speak, we would generate life and bring about the kind of change that world needs the most. It would be the God kind of change.

When we call people together it should be to hear the Word of God because no other matter is important enough to assemble people together in the house of God to hear. They don't need to hear what's going on in Washington, DC, They could get that from CNN or Fox. They need something that generates life, only God's word carries that impact.

- "Come and hear, all ye that fear God, and I will declare what he hath done for my soul." **(Ps 66:16 KJV)**

When we influence others by speaking God's word, we are creating a continuation for the life-giving word; our household would be blessed to live in an environment that speaks freely God's word.

The following scriptures demonstrate the ways the mouth should be used and contents of what one could use to express his or her feelings toward the Lord.

- **"My mouth shall shew forth thy righteousness and thy salvation all the day; for I know not the numbers thereof.**
- **I will go in the strength of the Lord GOD: I will make mention of thy righteousness, even of thine only." (Ps 71:15-16 KJV)**
- **"My lips shall greatly rejoice when I sing unto thee; and my soul, which thou hast redeemed.**
- **24 My tongue also shall talk of thy righteousness all the day long: for they are con-**

founded, for they are brought unto shame, that seek my hurt." (Ps 71:23-72:1 KJV) "Which we have heard and known, and our fathers have told us.

- **4 We will not hide them from their children, shewing to the generation to come the praises of the LORD, and his strength, and his wonderful works that he hath done." (Ps 78:3-4 KJV)**
- **"Sing unto him, sing psalms unto him: talk ye of all his wondrous works." (Ps 105:2 KJV)**
- **"With my lips have I declared all the judgments of thy mouth." (Ps 119:13 KJV)**

The soul that uses his or her mouth to promote the right cause will be continually blessed. It is not for us to know how many people we help, encourage, advice, inspire or influence. We just need to do what we do with the right motive. God is well able to credit our account with the right reward. His eyes are upon us and His ears are opened to our voices.

- "The lips of the righteous feed many: but fools die for want of wisdom." (Prov 10:21 KJV)
- "A wholesome tongue is a tree of life: but perverseness therein is a breach in the spirit." (Prov 15:4 KJV)
- "The lips of the wise disperse knowledge: but the heart of the foolish doeth not so." (Prov 15:7 KJV)

The lips of the wise are constantly busy giving out words that would benefit the lives of the hearers. They don't have time for foolishness, that assignment is carried out by the other group. The wise are happy only when the Lord is using their talent to glorify His name and build up His people.

Things that are dangerous are usually identified by a warning sign. Wouldn't it be nice if such was done for the mouth that was full of foolishness? Using that method could give others a head start in avoiding the threat of danger.

The Word of God marks the mouth of the wise by telling us what to expect. Those of us that want to be influenced by such wisdom and kindness would seek out such a mouth.

- "The wise man is known by his common sense, and a pleasant teacher is the best.
- 22 Wisdom is a fountain of life to those possessing it, but a fool's burden is his folly.
- 23 From a wise mind comes careful and persuasive speech.
- 24 Kind words are like honey-enjoyable and healthful." (Prov 16:21-24 TLB)

Kind words are like magic. They are known to attract attention from the least to the greatest. The effect that kind word has on the heart of the person needing them is like medicine. It brings healing within.

There is no substitute for right words. When I say right words, I am talking about words inspired by the Lord or words from the Holy Book. They are words that bring life and freshness to the souls of men.

- "Pay attention and listen to the sayings of the wise;
- apply your heart to what I teach,
- 18 for it is pleasing when you keep them in your heart

- **and have all of them ready on your lips." (Prov 22:17-18 (from NIV)**

We could call a mouth loaded with God's words and wisdom and knowledge, a beautiful mouth. The reason we could use that description is due to the value that it would carry. The fact that is, it stands ready to pass on helpful information, inspiration and courage.

When God's inspired word or words are spoken over a person fresh life is passed upon that person. When one is uplifted in the Word of God, he or she could do things then that he or she wouldn't otherwise attempt.

God instructed His priesthood to speak a word of encouragement and inspiration over His people; such words are found in the word in more than one place.

- **"And the LORD spake unto Moses, saying,**
- **23 Speak unto Aaron and unto his sons, saying, On this wise ye shall bless the children of Israel, saying unto them,**
- **24 The LORD bless thee, and keep thee:**

- **25 The LORD make his face shine upon thee, and be gracious unto thee:**
- **26 The LORD lift up his countenance upon thee, and give thee peace." (Num 6:22-26 KJV)**

It would be good if we believed that the words we speak had life and power. We often say to people: "**The Lord bless you.**" The words are right, but do we believe that our contact with the Lord gives us the authority to assure that the person would be blessed?

Don't we want people blessed and kept by the power of God? We want the Lord to look upon them with favor. We should want it to happen, and we should believe that we are speaking in line with the will of God because what we are saying is definitely according to the will of the Lord.

- **"And behold, Boaz came from Bethlehem, and said unto the reapers, The LORD be with you. And they answered him, The LORD bless thee." (Ruth 2:4 KJV)**
- **"The LORD that made heaven and earth bless thee out of Zion." (Ps 134:3 KJV)**

- "The grace of our Lord Jesus Christ be with you all. Amen." (Phil 4:23 KJV)

VOICE ACTIVATION

We could be sure that we were not given a tongue and a voice for naught. The Lord expects us to us this powerful life promoting instruments to the glory of His name and energizing of the supernatural.

The Bible list many ways and times that the voice was used to put in motion miracles and deliverances.

The Bible is a book that is loaded with facts. They are true facts, but we must learn how to activate those facts into actions. I say that the voice is one of the keys to transmitting these facts into deeds. When we employ our voices in faith, we convert our tongues into creative forces, we would be acting upon what we believe. It is not enough to believe, we must learn to release what we believe by speaking it forth.

If you would take the time to examine the scriptures you would find that many of the miracles that took place were preceded using the voice. These facts are recorded so that we would get the revelation that the mouth plays a major role in the release of the supernatural.

We know that the children of Israel marched around the Jericho walls six times and then seven times on the seventh day, but the wall didn't come down until they shouted with their voices. If you should wonder why the walls didn't fall until after they cried out, my answer would be voice activation is God's way. When it is employed it moves God into action when God start moving, the supernatural commences to take place.

Let us take a look at the word <u>activate</u>: to make active; cause to function or act.

Synonyms: actuate, animate, arouse charge, energize, impel, prompt, raise, rouse, spark, start, and mobilize.

After the children of Israel finished marching, it was then time to activate their miracle through the use of the voice. The Lord told Joshua in advance that

He had given them the city, but they didn't receive entrance into the city until they had cried or shouted with their voices.

- **"And the second day they compassed the city once, and returned into the camp: so they did six days.**
- **15 And it came to pass on the seventh day, that they rose early about the dawning of the day, and compassed the city after the same manner seven times: only on that day they compassed the city seven times.**
- **16 And it came to pass at the seventh time, when the priests blew with the trumpets, Joshua said unto the people, Shout; for the LORD hath given you the city." (Josh 6:14-16 KJV)**

Make no mistake, the Bible is not saying they danced, they shouted with their voices. You dance with your feet and shout with your voice.

Shout: to utter a sudden loud cry; to utter in a loud voice; to command attention as if by shouting;

to speak or utter in a loud distinct carrying voice. (Franklin Language Master)

We know that they didn't shout the walls down; they activated the supernatural by releasing their faith with their voices.

It is quite interesting to notice that the people were instructed to maintain silence for the first six days of marching. They were also silent on the seventh day, and they were silent until their course of action had been completed. God didn't want them to waste their energy in a way that nothing would be accomplished. In other words, He didn't want them to waste words.

The Lord gives us a hint in the book of James: **"Wherefore, my beloved brethren, let every man be swift to hear, slow to speak," (James 1:19 KJV)**

We could say that the march around the Jericho walls was an act of obedience. After they finished obeying, the time had come for a miracle. To make that happen, God allowed them to employ their voices.

- **"So the people shouted when the priests blew with the trumpets: and it came to pass, when the people heard the sound of the trumpet, and the people shouted with a great shout, that the wall fell down flat, so that the people went up into the city, every man straight before him, and they took the city." (Josh 6:20 KJV)**

This was a wonderful combination employed by the children of Israel. First of all, they acted in child like obedience, rising up each morning for six days and quietly marching around the city. After their march was complete, the activated the supernatural by obeying the command to shout.

It is common knowledge that the Lord could work without us but that is not His plan. The role that He wants us to play oftentimes is so simple that failure to walk in faith would cause us to miss out.

We see nowhere that doing the march around the walls of Jericho that anyone asked, why are we doing this. Alternatively, I don't see any need for all of this silence or marching. They just obeyed and marched on. When it was time to shout, I believe they all shouted. After they did what they were told to do, then the Lord did what He does best, and that is supernaturally moved.

In the book of Judges, we have yet another miraculous occurrence that followed the use of the voice. We are familiar with the Gideon three hundred man army, but rarely do we hear the emphasis placed on the fact that they activated their miracle with their voices.

We know about Gideon's procedure of elimination of his vast army as he was instructed by the Lord; however, when you calculate the enemy's armies, it seems that his was too small to start with.

Let us keep in mind when God gets ready to perform a miracle. He doesn't expect us to have the wherewithal. He just wants us to trust and obey Him, and He can take it from there.

It is faith building to observe the strategy that the Lord uses to work a miracle with this small army of believing men.

The Lord doesn't expect us to draw our faith out of the sky but out of His word. When His word is spoken, it has the power to feed one's faith.

- **"And when Gideon was come, behold, there was a man that told a dream unto**

> his fellow, and said, Behold, I dreamed a dream, and, lo, a cake of barley bread tumbled into the host of Midian, and came unto a tent, and smote it that it fell, and overturned it, that the tent lay along.
> - **14 And his fellow answered and said, This is nothing else save the sword of Gideon the son of Joash, a man of Israel: for into his hand hath God delivered Midian, and all the host.**
> - **15 And it was so, when Gideon heard the telling of the dream, and the interpretation thereof, that he worshipped, and returned into the host of Israel, and said, Arise; for the LORD hath delivered into your hand the host of Midian." (Judg 7:13-15 KJV)**

After Gideon heard the interpretation of this soul sustaining vision, he was ready to take on the enemy.

I would like to say, that after you and I hear God's word, we should be primed to face whatever life sends our way, because the living Word of God contains everything we need to move us toward Him and usher in the supernatural.

The next few verses contain the strategy that the Lord gave Gideon. It was all he needed, and his next move to activate the supernatural was to obey.

- **"He divided the three hundred men into three groups and gave each man a trumpet and a clay jar with a torch in it. Then he explained his plan.**
- **"When we arrive at the outer guardposts of the camp," he told them, "do just as I do. As soon as I and the men in my group blow our trumpets, you blow yours on all sides of the camp and shout, 'We fight for God and for Gideon!'"**
- **19 It was just after midnight and the change of guards when Gideon and the hundred men with him crept to the outer edge of the camp of Midian.**
- **Suddenly, they blew their trumpets and broke their clay jars so that their torches blazed into the night. Then the other two hundred of his men did the same, blowing the trumpets in their right hands, and holding the flaming torches in their left**

> **hands, all shouting, "For the Lord and for Gideon!"**
> - **21 Then they just stood and watched as the whole vast enemy army began rushing around in a panic, shouting and running away. 22 For in the confusion the Lord caused the enemy troops to begin fighting and killing each other from one end of the camp to the other, and they fled into the night to places as far away as Beth-shittah near Zererah, and to the border of Abel-meholah near Tabbath." (Judg 7:16-22 TLB)**

It is moving to see such a wonderful display of the supernatural following such a simple plan. That goes to show that when we do thing's God's way, we are sure to overcome great odds. That is why the Lord wanted Gideon's army reduced. He wanted them to know after it was all over that it was the Lord's doing and not just human effort.

They had a part to play, but their part was plain and simple. They needed to follow the instructions, as they were given by Gideon and in the end they shouted with their voices. When they shouted, the enemy became confused and started to destroy one another. I believe we could get rid of some of the mind- baffling soul-vexing heart-stressing spirits, if we would learn to use our voices.

- **"Then the other two hundred of his men did the same, blowing the trumpets in their right hands, and holding the flaming torches in their left hands, <u>all shouting</u>, "For the Lord and for Gideon!"**

We see that they activated their miracle by using their voices. It may not have made sense but it sure made the enemy turn on each other. The army of Gideon didn't have to fight. They believed, obeyed and shouted with their voices, God took over, and the enemy took off.

This supernatural action was so significant that the Lord allowed another account similar to this one to take place; it too was recorded, so we could be encouraged to use our voices.

- **"As the people from every part of Judah stood before the Lord with their little ones, wives, and children, 14 the Spirit of the**

Lord came upon one of the men standing there-Jahaziel (son of Zechariah, son of Benaiah, son of Jeiel, son of Mattaniah the Levite, who was one of the sons of Asaph).

- **15 "Listen to me, all you people of Judah and Jerusalem, and you, O king Jehoshaphat!" he exclaimed. "The Lord says, 'Don't be afraid! Don't be paralyzed by this mighty army! For the battle is not yours, but God's!"(2 Chron 20:13-15 TLB)**

God uses the same pattern that He used to encourage Gideon. He sent His word to inspire faith and hope in the hearts of His children. The Word of God plays a major role in every supernatural occurrence.

Jehoshaphat and Israel heard the exact words they need to hear. They heard words to remind them that it was God's battle: **"For the battle is not yours, but God's!"** Since it was God's battle, they had a right to expect the Lord to take over and do what He had done for others, and what He does best. Putting the enemy to flight is one of the things He is known to do.

God will always do His part, and He expects His children to do their part. Believe, speak and act, in this account. They used their voices to praise the Lord.

- **"After consultation with the leaders of the people, he determined that there should be a choir leading the march, clothed in sanctified garments and singing the song "His Loving-kindness Is Forever" as they walked along praising and thanking the Lord! 22 And at the moment they began to sing and to praise, the Lord caused the armies of Ammon, Moab, and Mount Seir to begin fighting among themselves, and they destroyed each other! 23 For the Ammonites and Moabites turned against their allies from Mount Seir and killed every one of them. And when they had finished that job, they turned against each other! 24 So, when the army of Judah arrived at the watchtower that looks out over the wilderness, as far as they could look there were dead bodies lying on the**

ground-not a single one of the enemy had escaped." (2 Chron 20:21-24 TLB)

You notice that fighting God's battle His way requires some unusual action. The battles that we wage are against an uncommon enemy. The enemy that is out to get us uses people to get next us. You notice there were nations united against Israel, they wanted to bring about their defeat. You can be sure that the Devil was the promoter if that idea. Anyone or anything that the Lord God shows special interest in, the Devil is opposed to that person or thing and would do anything within his power to bring that person or thing down. That is the only technique he feels would touch the Lord where it would hurt the most. His hatred for the Lord and his knowledge of God's love for His people gives him all the more reason to attack and attack with vengeance.

As you know, Israel was despised by all the nations of the earth, this was not normal it was demonic and yet was, because Satan wants to try and punish our God.

When King Jehoshaphat consulted with the people, they organized ways to activate the power of God. They knew long ago that God dwells in the midst of praise, so they arranged to put the singers and praiser ahead of the army. Since it was God's battle, they decided to give Him what He works with best; they prepared to offer Him praise.

- **"And Jehoshaphat bowed his head with his face to the ground: and all Judah and the inhabitants of Jerusalem fell before the LORD, worshipping the LORD.**
- **19 And the Levites, of the children of the Kohathites, and of the children of the Korhites, stood up to praise the LORD God of Israel with a loud voice on high."(2 Chron 20:18-19 KJV)**

We understand that loud noises don't scare the devil and his kind off, but it sure will activate the promises of God and keep the praiser from succumbing to depression, fear and defeat.

I will say that the Lord expects His children to come before Him with loud noise because He commanded it. If one does what the Lord wants and expect, he or she would make a loud noise unto the Lord.

"And when he had consulted with the people, he appointed singers unto the LORD, and that should praise the beauty of holiness, as they went out before the army, and to say, Praise the LORD; for his mercy endureth for ever." (2 Chron 20:21 KJV)

A faithless person could notice their mode of operation and would quickly express the idea that putting the singers and praiser ahead of the army doesn't make sense. They wouldn't know that one operating in faith doesn't have to make sense. All he or she would have to do is believe God and follow His lead.

Just between me and my readers, there are many things in the Bible that doesn't make sense, but they sure do make a way for a miracle.

It didn't make sense to tell the sun to stand still, but it stopped until the children of Israel could finish of the enemy. It didn't make sense to store a man in a whale's belly for three days and night but its symbolic message is yet saying, that in due time the Lord will raise you up. It didn't make sense to tell about a boy with two fish and five biscuits when there were more than five thousand men to be fed, but it sure did make a meal.

So we can't give up because a thing doesn't make sense. When things make sense, it is a good chance you won't need faith. When we need a miracle, making sense won't cause a change, but having faith will.

I would like to go on record as saying the greater one's need is, the louder that person should cry, holler, scream, yell, utter or cry out. This would be for his or her use or a display that he or she is really serious and is not willing to take no for an answer.

The blind men in the gospel books serve as typical examples of what I am talking about. They cried to get Jesus' attention but were told to hush. Since they knew what they had come for, they just raised their volume so that the crowed would not drown out their voices.

- **"And, behold, two blind men sitting by the way side, when they heard that Jesus passed by, cried out, saying, Have mercy on us, O Lord, thou Son of David. And the multitude rebuked them, because they should hold their peace: but they cried the**

more, saying, Have mercy on us, O Lord, thou Son of David." (Matt 20:30-31KJV)

The plea of these blind men was with great intensity because they really wanted to see. They knew that Jesus gained a reputation as one that could cause the blind to see, they wanted to see.

The people that could see didn't share such burden; therefore, they wanted them to shut up. Notice, Dear Readers, it was not Jesus that told them to hold their peace or shut up. It was the people that could see, but couldn't understand the intensity in which they pursued the Master.

Take a guess, what would have happened had those men listen to the crowd? Would they have gone home seeing or blind? That is why we don't need to let others dictate what we need the Lord to do for us? I don't think we need to tone our voices to suit the feelings of others. The Lord said make a joyful noise and the people that can't stand much noise had better not follow us to heaven, because there will be plenty noise up there.

The men kept crying and the Lord started calling for them to be brought to Him. They wouldn't have received such an invitation had they kept their mouth shut. You may be inches from a blessing, so open your mouth to the Lord.

- **"And Jesus stood still, and called them, and said, What will ye that I shall do unto you?**
- **33 They say unto him, Lord, that our eyes may be opened.**
- **34 So Jesus had compassion on them, and touched their eyes: and immediately their eyes received sight, and they followed him." (Matt 20:32-21:1 KJV)**

Please notice, when the Master made His call for the men to come, that call didn't include any of the "be quiet" supporters. He wanted to support someone that knew that he or she should make a joyful noise to the Lord.

You could be sure that the enemy is not against noise. He just doesn't want it to be made unto the Lord. You can make all the noise you please at the arenas, ballparks and football stadiums, but he wants you to tone it down when you are in a place of public worship. It doesn't take all that emotionalism, don't you know that the Lord is intelligent?

When we engage in the things that the Lord commands, we always come out on the blessed end. The main problem is, too few are consistent in carrying out the laws of God.

You could be sure that the Lord knows clearly the purpose of His people rejoicing in an excitable fashion. He knows that the other side of rejoicing is where the sad, depressed and unhappy dwell. He does not want His children in that camp.

When we engage in the act of enthusiasm, we activate the power of God. The Bible is supportive in the fact that many of the miracles that took place in the Bible were preceded by exhilarating shouts.

- **"Make a joyful noise unto the LORD, all ye lands." (Ps 100:1 KJV)**
- **"Enter into his gates with thanksgiving, and into his courts with praise: be thankful unto him, and bless his name." (Ps 100:4 KJV)**

LET YOUR VOICE BE HEARD

If we should listen to the enemy or some of his supporters, we would get the feeling that crying out has no merits. Looking at the Word of God, one must be impressed that Bible supports crying.

The Lord tells His believing children to cry. He tells us that He is listening, and that He will deliver.

The testimonies that are on record were left to inspire faith in the heart of the readers. We should take the attitude, if the Lord did it before, He can do it again. If He did it for someone else, He will do it for me. When we take that approach we are acting in faith and our faith is sure to be rewarded.

Let us not confuse the method of crying that the Bible speaks of with what we are accustomed to calling crying. We are not talking about the release of water from the tear ducts, we are talking about a sound coming out of your mouth.

- **"I cried unto the LORD with my voice, and he heard me out of his holy hill. Selah." (Ps 3:4 KJV)**
- **"This poor man cried, and the LORD heard him, and saved him out of all his troubles." (Ps 34:6 KJV)**
- **"I cried unto God with my voice, even unto God with my voice; and he gave ear unto me." (Ps 77:1 KJV)**
- **"Thou hast heard my voice: hide not thine ear at my breathing, at my cry." (Lam 3:56 KJV)**

The preceding verses leave no doubt about crying. It is the voice that we should use when we want to engage action or get attention and help from the Lord.

Only the Devil and his kind are opposed to one crying out. The enemy has seen too may of God's crying children delivered from his control, afflictions and troubles. He knows the Lord will deliver them that cry, but he hopes we never discover it or put it to practice. The Devil knows if he can't shut us up, he can't hold us down. That is why he tries to overload us with burdens, cares, stress, pressure, heartache, pain, disappointment, etc. The devil brings these things upon us to shut us down. He wants us to feel that our plea is going unheard.

That is why we must keep on looking in the book of books and get the Lord's word on a matter, and then put to practice what we learn. If the Bible says cry, we should cry. When the Bible says shout unto the Lord, we should open wide our mouth and release the strongest cry we could make.

We noticed in an earlier verse that a poor man cried and was heard, we should feel that if the Lord heard one, He is capable of hearing another: **"This poor man cried, and the LORD heard him"**

The Lord is daily watching His children, He is also listening for their cry. When we cry, He is sure to hear us. Just remember, it is our duty and privilege to cry, and it is the Lord's responsibility to hear and to deliver. The Lord is known for doing His business with efficiency.

The following verses, I trust, will serve as a reminder that crying is in order and will not go unheard or answered.

- **"The eyes of the LORD are upon the righteous, and his ears are open unto their cry." (Ps 34:15 KJV)**
- **"The righteous cry, and the LORD heareth, and delivereth them out of all their troubles." (Ps 34:17 KJV)**
- **"Many are the afflictions of the righteous: but the LORD delivereth him out of them all." (Ps 34:19 KJV)**

We have God's word on the fact that afflictions are common in the believing family, so is deliverance. In fact, they are delivered out of them all: **"but the LORD delivereth him out of them all."**

Deliverance is promised and should be expected by the children of God. We should know that just as the enemy brings afflictions our Lord brings deliverance. We should keep our focus on what the Lord does and not let the enemy distract our attention with his lies.

- "He shall deliver thee in six troubles: yea, in seven there shall no evil touch thee." (Job 5:19 KJV)
- "These things I have spoken unto you, that in me ye might have peace. In the world ye shall have tribulation: but be of good cheer; I have overcome the world." (John 16:33 KJV)
- "Confirming the souls of the disciples, and exhorting them to continue in the faith, and that we must through much tribulation enter into the kingdom of God." (Acts 14:22 KJV)
- "For our light affliction, which is but for a moment, worketh for us a far more exceeding and eternal weight of glory;" (2 Cor 4:17 KJV)

When our troubles seems more than we can bear, we have God's word on what to do. We are not left unprotected, if we would call on or cry out to the Lord we are assured that we would be heard and delivered.

When we are faithful in offering to Him thanksgiving and praise, we should be inspired to believe that He would be faithful in delivering us. That is why I emphasize the importance of activating the supernatural by using the voice. We should keep praise on our lips, and this would keep us from murmuring and complaining.

- **"Offer unto God thanksgiving; and pay thy vows unto the most High:**
- **15 And call upon me in the day of trouble: I will deliver thee, and thou shalt glorify me." (Ps 50:14-15 KJV)**

The Lord tells the future victim of trouble to pay his vows by offering unto Him thanksgiving, and after he has done that, when his day of trouble comes, he should call upon the Lord.

This is a very gracious invitation offered to the one that is attacked by trouble. The Lord wants us to call Him, He didn't say call your mother, father, or preacher. He said call upon Him. He tells us before we make the call what will happen, He said that He would deliver. He also tells what the delivered should do, **"and thou shalt glorify me."** That seem like a small price to pay for deliverance; however, not all are willing to conform to giving thanks.

Multitudes have been blessed and delivered by the Lord, but acted as if they deserved what they got or that the Lord should have done more. The spirit of ingratitude has almost drowned this world. This ungrateful spirit has been around for some time and has only gotten worse.

In Jesus' day, the ratio of gratitude appeared to be one out of ten. He healed ten men of leprosy, but only one returned to say thank you. It stands to reason that if it was that low in Jesus' day, only the Lord knows how low it is today.

To change the degree of gratitude, when the Lord delivers you, please make sure that you offer unto Him Thanksgiving and praise. That is a small price pay for any act of God.

The outlook of faith says that the only reason I don't receive deliverance would be if I didn't call unto the Lord. If I don't call Him, He is under no obligation to act because He told me to call Him in the day of trouble.

Let's look at the word trouble: to agitate mentally or spiritually: disturb, worry. To put to inconvenience, to afflict. (Franklin Language Master)

I think that all of us are good at recognizing natural trouble; however, we have a tendency to ignore or disregard spiritual trouble. That is the one that could do us the most harm and send us in the direction we don't need to go.

The Lord has given us the plan. All we have to do is work it according to His word and it would work every time and for all that believe. **"And call upon me in the day of trouble: I will deliver thee, and thou shalt glorify me."** After we have offered unto the Lord thanksgiving and praise, we can expect Him to work deliverance and after He delivers, He expects us to glorify Him.

The Lord is big on His people offering thanksgiving. He expects it to be done and we should gladly do it because He is worthy to be praised.

- **"Oh that men would praise the LORD for his goodness, and for his wonderful works to the children of men!" (Ps 107:8 KJV)**
  "Oh that men would praise the LORD for his goodness, and for his wonderful works to the children of men!" (Ps 107:15 KJV)
  "Oh that men would praise the LORD for his goodness, and for his wonderful works to the children of men!" (Ps 107:21 KJV)

- **"Oh that men would praise the LORD for his goodness, and for his wonderful works to the children of men!" (Ps 107:31 KJV)**

The Lord leaves no doubt about what He expects out of those He works wonders for. He expects them to give thanks for His wonderful works. The thing is that the Lord wants to be very clear, He purposed to make it clear. That is why He repeats what He wants a few times over.

The Lord yet expects us to call upon Him in the day of trouble; He just wants us to know what we should do after being the beneficiary of His wonderful works.

The good thing about His invitation is there are no limits placed on the call such as, who, why or when. He just said call in the day of trouble. He didn't say what kind of trouble it has to be, I take it that means any forms of trouble.

The Lord in His word supports that He stands ready to help all that need help no matter who they are or what kind of help they need. The thing that stands between the needy and the help that is needed is a cry.

- **"For he shall deliver the needy when he crieth; the poor also, and him that hath no helper." (Ps 72:12 KJV)**

The Lord also promised to accompany the ones that cry. He promised that if they are in trouble, that He will be in there with them and where the Spirit of the Lord is, there is liberty.

- **"Because he hath set his love upon me, therefore will I deliver him: I will set him on high, because he hath known my name.**
- **He shall call upon me, and I will answer him: I will be with him in trouble; I will deliver him, and honour him." (Ps 91:14-15 KJV)**

Notice where the Lord said He would be when we were in trouble. It would be good to have Him come to us after trouble, but He said that He would be with the believer in trouble. The record will show that He is true to His claim. When they Hebrew boys in the fiery finance. Since they wouldn't bow; He made sure that they wouldn't burn.

- "Then was Nebuchadnezzar full of fury, and the form of his visage was changed against Shadrach, Meshach, and Abed-nego: therefore he spake, and commanded that they should heat the furnace one seven times more than it was wont to be heated.
- And he commanded the most mighty men that were in his army to bind Shadrach, Meshach, and Abed-nego, and to cast them into the burning fiery furnace.
- Then these men were bound in their coats, their hosen, and their hats, and their other garments, and were cast into the midst of the burning fiery furnace.
- Therefore because the king's commandment was urgent, and the furnace exceeding hot, the flame of the fire slew those men that took up Shadrach, Meshach, and Abed-nego.
- And these three men, Shadrach, Meshach, and Abed-nego, fell down bound into the midst of the burning fiery furnace.
- Then Nebuchadnezzar the king was astonied, and rose up in haste, and spake, and said unto his counsellers, Did not we cast

> **three men bound into the midst of the fire? They answered and said unto the king, True, O king.**
> - **He answered and said, Lo, I see four men loose, walking in the midst of the fire, and they have no hurt; and the form of the fourth is like the Son of God." (Dan 3:19-25 KJV)**

The Lord made good His word. He got in the furnace with His servants because they took the right stand. They didn't let what everybody else was doing influence them to follow the crowd. They got in trouble, but they served a God that was not a stranger to trouble, and He had promised to be their refuge.

I can happily say that His promise extends to us. It would be to our advantage to capitalize on God's wonderful offers to call upon Him in trouble, because they are sure to come as long as we live in this world. As long as you maintain a love for the Lord, you can be sure that the enemy of the Lord's, your adversary, will make sure that your life will encounter difficulties.

We don't have to seek for trouble, it is known to seek after the godly. All we have to do is live godly and trouble will surely come our way. However, we are blessed to have someone that is qualified when it comes to dealing with trouble. If we would call Him, He will deliver and when He delivers, we should express our gratitude by offering Him thanks.

> OTHER BOOKS BY BISHOP CLIFTON JONES, THESE BOOKS MAY BE ORDERED IN THE FOLLOWING WAYS:
> CHECK OUT OUR WEB SITE: jtchurch.com
> JERUSALEM TEMPLE CHURCH
> 414 IVY STREET
> PHILADELPHIA, MS 39350
> 601-562-3703
> 601-259-2412
> 601-416-2632 CELL
> E-MAIL: cliftonbcj@aol.com   FAX: 601-656-9645
> Mayfrancesjones@aol.com

YOU MAY MAIL ORDER ANY OF OUR MATERIAL BY WRITING US AT

JERUSALEM CHURCH 414 IVY STREET PHILADELPHIA, MS. 39350

DON'T FORGET OUR WEB-SITE@ JTCHURCH.COM

PRAYER CLINIC MANUAL
FAITH CLINIC MANUAL
LORD HEAL ME FROM THE INSIDE
HOW TO KEEP THE DEVIL OUT OF YOUR
  BUSINESS
I THOUGHT IT WAS THE DEVIL BUT IT WAS
  ME TOO

FASTING AND PRAYER FOR CHANGE
IT'S ALL ABOUT LOVE
A LITTLE KINDLING FOR YOUR FIRE
YOU NEED TO GROW UP
TOUGH FAITH
SOBER ADVICE FOR LAST DAY LIVING
FALLING IN THE WRONG PLACES
DYING AT THE DOCTORS DOOR
MISTAKING IDENTITY
ARE YOU INDICTING ME?
PRAYER CLINIC WORKBOOK
FAITH CLINIC WORKBOOK
RUT OR REVIVAL
UNDER ATTACK BUT EQUIPPED TO STAND
IS IT OLD FASHION OR SAFE
    SANCTIFICATION?
GOD'S MEDICINE FOR THE WHOLE FAMILY
HOW PREACHERS COMMIT SUCIDE
HOLINESS TEACHING IN UNHOLY TIMES
A REQUEST FOR DIVINE INSPECTION
RAPED IN THE PRESENCE OF WITNESSES

Breinigsville, PA USA
24 May 2010
238576BV00002B/2/P